The Which? Guide to the Energy-Saving Home

About the author

Ruth Turner is a freelance journalist and author who has contributed to a variety of specialist publications, writing on environmental, political and transport-related issues.

Acknowledgements

Many people have provided invaluable help in the preparation of this book. The author and publishers would especially like to thank Delroy Corinaldi, Sandie Edwards, Julie Mendis, Lindsey Smith and Rosemary Ward at Consumers' Association; Bob Harrison and Simon Leach at ITS Research & Testing Centre; Helen Beardsley, Kelly Butler, Tim Curtis and Mark Williamson at the Energy Saving Trust; David Hoadley at Solent Energy Efficiency Advice Centre; Julia Green at Energy Inform; Dr Abubakr Bahaj at the University of Southampton; David Davies, David Holloway, Kim Lewis, Penney Poyzer and Brian Price.

Sue Freeman and Wendy Garlick at Consumers' Association, Paul Sterlini at Understanding Energy, and Maddy Harland, editor of *Permaculture* magazine, also gave us assistance with the book.

Copyright permissions

We are very grateful to the following people and organisations for giving us permission to use the material detailed below.

Energy Inform. The comparative table of electrical appliances on page 88 was supplied from the forthcoming edition of *The Energy Advice Handbook*.

The Energy Saving Trust. The information on draught-proofing and insulation in Chapter 3 is based on its booklet *The DIY Guide to Energy Efficiency*.

Penney Poyzer. The picture of the Nottingham Ecohome on page 158 is reproduced from her website.

Understanding Energy educational service. The information on energy sources in Chapter 2 is based on its on-line resource *The Energy Files*.

The Which? Guide to the Energy-Saving Home

Ruth Turner

 CONSUMERS' ASSOCIATION

Which? Books are commissioned and researched by
Consumers' Association and published by
Which? Ltd, 2 Marylebone Road, London NW1 4DF
Email: books@which.net

Distributed by The Penguin Group:
Penguin Books Ltd, 80 Strand, London WC2R 0RL

First edition May 2003

Copyright © 2003 Which? Ltd

British Library Cataloguing in Publication Data
A catalogue record for this book is available from the British Library

ISBN 0 85202 909 8

For a full list of Which? books, please call 0800 252100, access our website at www.which.net, or write to Which? Books, PO Box 44, Hertford SG14 1SH. A selection of available titles is listed at the back of this book.

Editorial and production: Alethea Doran, Robert Gray, Nithya Rae, Ian Robinson, Mary Sunderland, Barbara Toft
Original cover concept by Sarah Harmer
Cover photograph by Mauritius, ace photoagency

Typeset by Saxon Graphics Ltd, Derby
Printed and bound in England by Clays Ltd, St Ives plc

Contents

★ An asterisk next to the name of an organisation in the text indicates that its address
or contact details can be found in this section

Foreword

Energy efficiency rarely makes the headlines. But it is really important news. If you make your home more energy efficient, you save money and help the environment. So it is a win-win situation.

Look around. Climate change is already affecting us. Seven of the ten warmest years on record occurred in the last decade, and heavy downpours now contribute twice as much rain as they did in the early 1960s. Climate change is likely to intensify. Ultimately it will affect everything, including agriculture, water resources, human health, wildlife and the countryside – both in Britain and across the world.

The production and use of electricity, gas, coal and oil releases a vast amount of carbon dioxide into the atmosphere. That carbon dioxide is building up above the earth creating a greenhouse effect, which is warming the planet and causing changes in our climate.

It's as simple as this: the more energy we consume, the more it costs us, and the more we are damaging our environment and jeopardising the future for generations to come. Which is why it is extremely important that we all do out bit for the environment by being more energy efficient.

It is easy to save energy. If you have cavity walls, you can have them insulated without any work or disruption inside your house and, for a average semi-detached house, the cost will be paid for by reduced energy use in about three years. Small changes in our everyday activities can be equally effective. Think about this: if everyone boiled only the water they needed to make a cup of tea instead of filling the kettle every time, we could save enough electricity to run practically all the street lighting in the country.

I hope this guide will give you the encouragement and provide you with the information necessary to help you take the first steps towards a more energy-efficient way of living.

Peter Lehmann
Chairman of the Energy Saving Trust

Introduction

Faced with environmental problems on a global scale, we can often feel powerless to make a difference. Most people are aware of the threat to our climate posed by the continued use of fossil fuels to generate power. They may even have experienced the effects of this in their own lives – for example, floods in recent winters. But to many the solution seems to lie with governments rather than individual consumers.

However, the potential for change through more efficient use of energy is enormous. In the UK Climate Change Programme the government has identified its commitments to help tackle global warming. It is estimated that 82 per cent of the programme's targets could be delivered through energy-efficiency measures alone. One reason for this is that much of the UK's housing stock (more than 40 per cent of which is over 60 years old) is of a poor quality and offers considerable scope for energy-efficiency improvements. In February 2003, in its long-awaited Energy White Paper, the government declared a target of a 60 per cent cut in carbon dioxide emissions by 2050. And the Trade and Industry Secretary, Patricia Hewitt, said that energy efficiency was the 'cheapest and simplest way of achieving our goals'.

This book presents practical advice on how to make energy-saving improvements to your home – and save money on utility bills – through proper insulation, draught-proofing and other measures. For example:

- the average UK home loses more than 40 per cent of its heat through the roof and walls. Insulating your loft and walls and fitting draught-proofing to doors and windows could save you up to £100 a year on your fuel bills

- over half of the energy used in our homes is for heating. By replacing a 15-year-old boiler with a new energy-efficient model, you could reduce your heating costs by between 20 and 40 per cent
- fitting a jacket to a hot-water tank can cut heat loss by up to 75 per cent
- if every UK household installed one energy-efficient light bulb, the carbon dioxide saved would fill the Royal Albert Hall nearly 3,000 times.

Electrical appliances, such as fridges, freezers or washing machines, offer further scope for energy saving. By buying A-rated energy-efficient models consumers can avoid unnecessary waste and expense. Savings can also be made by using 'brown goods' (TVs, DVDs and so on) more efficiently, largely by avoiding the energy-draining standby mode wherever possible.

In addition to reducing our consumption of energy, we can conserve energy by reducing, reusing or recycling household waste. Recycling uses less energy than producing goods from raw materials.

By encouraging more investment in renewable energy sources – such as wind, wave and solar power, which produce no carbon dioxide – we will help to secure a less environmentally damaging, more sustainable, power supply. The Renewables Obligation means that, in 2003, electricity suppliers must source at least 3 per cent of their power from renewable sources. Consumers can further support the development of these technologies by opting to buy electricity from a 'green' energy supplier.

According to a survey by the Energy Saving Trust, over 70 per cent of people in the UK want more information about how they can save energy. Whether you just want to draught-proof your windows or are an enthusiast who wants to install solar water-heating, *The Which? Guide to the Energy-Saving Home* is the place to start.

Chapter 1

The energy issue

Energy is an essential part of our everyday lives. We need it to heat and light our homes, run our transport system and manufacture goods. From wood and coal to oil, gas and electricity, modern sources of energy have offered enormous gains but unfortunately come with a hidden cost. Not only do we often fail to make efficient use of this energy, but power generation has given rise to huge environmental problems on a global scale (see 'Energy and the environment', below). Moreover, most conventional energy resources are finite – so sooner or later they are going to run out.

Energy efficiency is something that concerns us all. Faced with the large-scale cost and pollution implications of continuing reliance on existing resources, government bodies and local authorities are taking steps to address the problem, while consumer awareness of the energy issue is growing. This book explores the major concerns facing us today and outlines some simple measures that will help you as an individual to save money on your energy bills *and* conserve the environment.

Energy efficiency: a common cause

Conserving energy is a goal with a high level of public support. An opinion poll carried out on behalf of the Energy Saving Trust (EST)★ in 2002 showed that:

- 76 per cent of the UK population believed that the government should invest time and money developing new ways to reduce energy consumption
- 73 per cent wanted more information about *why* they should save energy

- 77 per cent wanted information about *how* they should save energy.

On a wider scale, the government has called for a 20 per cent improvement in energy efficiency by 2010, with a further 20 per cent improvement by 2020. It is now looking to alternative sources of energy, such as wind and wave power (see Chapter 2), and in 2002 introduced the Renewables Obligation, which calls for all gas and electricity suppliers to ensure that by 2010 at least 10 per cent of the energy they sell comes from renewable sources. Energy suppliers are also required, by the Energy Efficiency Commitment, to invest around £500 million in energy-efficiency schemes in their customers' homes by 2005, in the form of grants and cash-back schemes.

According to EST, in order to reach the 2010 target for improved efficiency in the UK, we must:

- insulate the walls of more than seven million homes and the lofts of six million houses
- install 25 million energy-efficient fridges and fridge-freezers, and 20 million energy-efficient washing machines and tumble-driers
- fit 100 million low-energy light bulbs
- plumb in 9 million new efficient boilers.

Nearly 30 per cent of the energy supplied in the UK is used in our homes, so it is clear that we can make a lot of difference at a domestic level. Throughout this book we supply a wealth of practical advice on becoming more energy efficient, and explain what you need to consider when buying, installing or adapting accessories and appliances in the home (see Chapters 3 and 4).

Energy and the environment

It is now generally acknowledged that burning 'fossil fuels' – coal, oil and gas, formed from decayed vegetation and marine life over millions of years – gives rise to increased levels of 'greenhouse gas' emissions, thought to cause global warming and permanent climate change. The release of sulphur dioxide and nitrogen oxides into the atmosphere can also cause acid rain, which damages the natural environment.

At the 1992 United Nations Earth Summit in Rio, governments around the world committed themselves to finding ways of reversing global warming. In 1997, in Kyoto, they agreed to adopt a set of targets on reducing carbon dioxide emissions. The UK undertook to make a 20 per cent reduction by 2010. To help meet this target we will have to find greener, more environmentally friendly ways of generating power, while increasing energy efficiency to prevent needless waste.

Global warming – why worry?

When fossil fuels are burned to generate electricity, gases such as carbon dioxide, methane and nitrous oxide are released. These trap heat in the atmosphere in the same way as glass traps heat in a greenhouse, and are therefore known as 'greenhouse gases'. Oceans and plants absorb a certain amount of them but they cannot cope with the hundreds of millions of tonnes of man-made emissions produced each year. The volume of greenhouse gas emissions depends on the type of fuel and the amount burned – coal usually produces more emissions than oil or gas, for example. Nuclear fuels and renewable sources produce negligible amounts of greenhouse gas, but nuclear fuels (see Chapter 2) give rise to other environmental concerns.

With increasing levels of greenhouse gases in the atmosphere, too much heat is trapped and the planet gets hotter. This phenomenon is called 'global warming'. The average world temperature is rising and high glaciers appear to be melting along with the permafrost (a soil layer that remains below freezing all year). Research by the Scott Polar Research Institute found that ice at the North Pole thinned by a third during the 1990s, releasing large quantities of trapped methane and further adding to the problem.

The Intergovernmental Panel on Climate Change (IPCC)* has predicted that, globally, we are likely to see an increase in extreme and unpredictable weather – more and bigger storms, hurricanes, floods and droughts – as the atmosphere becomes warmer.

Climate change in the UK

Global warming is likely to affect the UK just as much as it does far-flung parts of the world. Heavy flooding over the past few years suggests that we may already be experiencing early manifestations of the syndrome. The UK Climate Impacts Programme* reports that the following changes are likely by the 2080s.

- *The UK climate will become warmer* The effects will be greater in the south and east than in the north and west, and temperatures are likely to increase more in summer and autumn than winter and spring. The temperature of UK coastal waters will also increase, although not as rapidly as that of the land. High summer temperatures will become more frequent, while very cold winters will become increasingly rare.
- *Winters will become wetter and summers may become drier* The changes will be most marked in the south and east. Summer rainfall may decrease in this region by 50 per cent or more, and winter rainfall may increase by up to 30 per cent. Summer soil moisture may be reduced by 40 per cent or more over large parts of England.
- *Heavy winter rainfall and snowfall will become more frequent* Currently experienced around once every two years, this sort of extreme weather may increase by between 5 and 20 per cent.
- *Average wind speeds could rise* A 30 per cent increase in gales in Wales and southern England in winter is possible.
- *Sea levels will continue to rise around most of the UK's shoreline, threatening low-lying coastal areas* Levels may reach 26cm to 86cm above the current level in south-east England. Extreme sea levels will occur between 10 and 20 times more frequently than at present. Some 10,000 hectares of mudflats and salt marshes are at risk of inundation; many of these are both vital wildfowl reserves and natural sources of coastal protection.
- *Salt intrusion may affect much of the UK's agricultural land* This could be an even more serious consequence of sea encroachment than rising water levels. Half of the UK's premium agricultural land is less than 5m above sea level and a high proportion of this could become saline.

Carbon dioxide emissions

The most damaging greenhouse gas is carbon dioxide. It is produced in large quantities each year, mainly from burning fossil fuels to generate energy in power stations. Global deforestation has intensified the impact of these emissions, as trees and plants, which soak up carbon dioxide, have disappeared owing to increasing consumer demand for timber products.

The main sources of carbon dioxide emissions in the UK are power stations, industry, road transport and the domestic sector. Emissions of carbon dioxide increased ten-fold between 1900 and 1998, and today one-quarter of all carbon dioxide emissions comes from the energy we use to heat and light our homes and power our household appliances.

Domestic energy consumption in the UK

Despite the obvious impetus to conserve energy and save the planet, we demand increasing amounts of energy to power our lives in the 21st century.

Most energy consumed in the domestic sector is for space heating (58 per cent of all energy delivered to the home in 2000). The other major areas of domestic energy consumption are heating water, lighting, appliances and cooking.

According to the Department for Trade and Industry (DTI), between 1970 and 2000:

- domestic energy consumption increased by 32 per cent
- energy use by cold appliances (fridges, fridge-freezers, freezers) rose by 274 per cent
- energy consumption for lighting and appliances went up by 157 per cent.

Your own rate of energy consumption, and the ease with which you can put in place energy-saving measures, will depend on the size of your household, your lifestyle and the sort of building you inhabit. The average household could save around 2 tonnes of carbon dixoide emissions a year by improving energy efficiency. Saving energy will also help save money. Some measures are simple and low-cost; others require a more long-term commitment.

Electronic goods can eat up energy

The amount of electrical appliances bought in the UK has rocketed, and an increased number of households means greater demand for consumer goods. The biggest boom has been in the number of houses owning VCRs and fridge-freezers. Statistics show that 59 per cent of households own two or more televisions, and 14 per cent own two or more VCRs, while 13 per cent of households have acquired a DVD player since they were introduced in 1997. Home computers have become increasingly popular – 45 per cent of households owned one in 2000. Perhaps as a result of this rise in acquisition of products, the amount of energy used by appliances has increased by 9 per cent since 1990.

How old is your house?

The age and fabric of your house can affect how much energy you save or waste. In the UK, 40 per cent of the housing stock was built before 1945, 46 per cent between 1945 and 1984, and 14 per cent after 1984. Newer homes have to conform to much higher energy-efficiency standards than older buildings. In simple terms, heating a draughty old house is bound to prove more expensive than keeping a modern one warm. A number of houses are now being built that incorporate a very high level of energy efficiency into their design – Chapter 8 includes some examples of these. Most of us, however, live in older buildings that would benefit considerably from the implementation of some of the measures suggested in Chapter 3 of this book.

Obtaining an energy rating or energy check for your home

There are currently two methods of assessing homes to determine their energy efficiency – the Standard Assessment Procedure (SAP) and the National Home Energy Rating (NHER)★ scheme. The basis of both was a survey by the government's Building Research Establishment (BRE)★, which looked at hundreds of homes to discover their energy features, and then monitored them for up to two years to see how they performed in terms of temperatures, hot water consumption and fuel bills. From this data the government developed a Domestic Energy Model (BREDEM), which informs the SAP and NHER systems, although both scales use slightly different measurements.

The government's own scoring system, the SAP, operates on a scale from one (highly inefficient) to 100 (highly efficient). The SAP system looks only at the fixed elements of the home and is the same wherever the property is located in the UK. Therefore, all homes built to the same design should have exactly the same SAP rating. Since 1995 new homes have been required by law to have a SAP energy rating, so if you are buying a new home, remember to ask for this rating.

In 1990 the National Energy Foundation* launched the NHER scheme. This operates on a scoring system from nought to ten (the higher the score, the more energy-efficient your home is) and is a way of comparing the amount of fuel that would be used by different homes, assuming that the occupants live in them in the same way. The NHER model includes various location-specific elements – for example, whether the home is south-facing or sheltered from wind by other buildings – and so reflects actual running costs more closely. If two homes have the same floor area but different NHERs, then the home with the better (higher) NHER should cost less to run.

If you want an expert to carry out a detailed energy audit of your home, contact National Home Energy Rating* to find out if there is an assessor in your area. Alternatively you can contact your nearest Energy Efficiency Advice Centre (EEAC) – listed in the 'Useful contacts' section at the back of this book – which provide free advice to householders and small businesses. EEACs are staffed by expert energy advisors and offer a range of services to help consumers save energy, money and the environment.

An alternative to a full energy audit is a DIY Home Energy Check. This scheme, run by the EST, helps you identify where energy and money are being wasted in the home. It comprises a quick questionnaire which, when completed by you, allows your local EEAC to supply you with tailored reports pointing to the most cost-effective ways to save energy in your home. Your local centre will also tell you which grants are available in your area, and will give you details of local special offers as well as your nearest approved professional installers. (See Appendix II at the back of this book for details of some of the grants and offers available at the time of writing.)

Advice for low-income households

National Energy Action (NEA)* develops and promotes energy efficiency services to tackle the heating and insulation problems of low-income households. Working in partnership with central and local government, utilities companies, housing providers, consumer organisations and health services, NEA aims to eradicate fuel poverty (where households cannot afford to heat their homes – typically needing to spend 10 per cent or more of their income on basic energy needs) and campaigns for greater investment in energy efficiency to help those who are on low incomes or are vulnerable.

Becoming more energy-efficient

According to the Environment Agency*, there is huge scope to increase the efficiency of our energy and water use and to invest in more renewable energy supplies, but this will require a concerted effort from all sectors of the economy and from the general public. This means we need to change our habits in terms of how we use energy.

Saving energy in the home need not be difficult or expensive. For instance, a typical three-bedroom semi-detached house, without any insulation, might cost around £500 a year to heat. By following some simple energy-saving measures the household could cut its fuel bills by at least £100 a year without losing either warmth or comfort. (See Chapter 3 for practical advice on energy-saving measures.)

The main areas you need to consider are: insulation, heating and hot water, lighting and appliances. Below we outline some of the main things to think about – these subjects, along with other factors affecting energy usage, are covered in greater detail elsewhere in the book.

Insulation

In our homes, heat escapes mainly through 'fabric heat loss' or 'ventilation heat loss'. Fabric heat loss occurs when heat escapes through a part of the building structure which is exposed to the outside or to any other unheated space – for example, an unheated basement area or an unoccupied flat which is directly next door to an occupied one. Ventilation heat loss occurs when air flows in and out of a building through gaps in floorboards, doors and windows or through controlled ventilation such as air-bricks and grilles.

According to the Energy Saving Trust, more than 40 per cent of all the heat lost in an average home is through the roof and walls. Annually the amount of heat lost could be used to heat 3 million homes for a whole year.

Losing heat

The perils of not insulating your home are clear. Not only could you be shivering in a draughty house, but you face higher energy bills. Uninsulated homes typically show the following heat loss:

- 35 per cent goes through walls
- 25 per cent is lost through the roof
- 15 per cent is lost to draughts
- up to 15 per cent is lost through the floor
- 10 per cent is lost through windows.

Installing insulation can make a real difference, and it need not be expensive. Loft insulation alone can cut down energy usage (and heating bills) by 20 per cent, and hot-water tank insulation is a low-cost, easy-maintenance device now found in most houses.

These, along with cavity wall insulation and double glazing, are the main types of insulation in the UK. For more information see Chapter 3.

Heating and hot water

Over half of the average fuel bill results from heating and hot water. Older homes in particular are likely to have less energy-efficient heating systems than newer homes. By replacing an old boiler you could be saving over 20 per cent on your fuel bills, or up to 32 per cent if you change your existing boiler for a condensing boiler – considered to be the most efficient type (see Chapter 3). This may however be expensive initially.

If you are replacing your boiler, you should also consider upgrading your heating controls to maximise the efficiency of your heating system. By fitting new heating controls in addition to a condensing boiler you could save up to 40 per cent on your heating bills. By fitting an insulating jacket to your hot-water tank and lagging the hot-water pipes, you will waste even less energy and ensure that water stays hotter for longer periods. See Chapter 3 for more details.

Simple ways to save energy

Adopting a more energy-efficient lifestyle need not be difficult or expensive, and it is up to you how much effort you put into it. The following are just some examples of the no-cost or low-cost energy-saving measures described later in this book.

All around the house
- switch lights off in empty rooms
- close windows when the heating is on
- read your meters and compare readings to your bills
- Turn down the thermostat slightly (minimum 18°C)
- reduce heat loss by closing curtains at dusk
- put foil behind the radiators on external walls
- fill in the gaps between the skirting board and the floor, and draught-proof areas where heat escapes (window frames, doors, etc.)
- heat only the amount of water you will actually use
- turn your TV off at the set rather than leaving it on standby
- turn off your computer when it is not in use
- use modern electric storage heaters if you are in an all-electric home
- use low-energy light bulbs
- move your furniture away from radiators to allow heat to circulate more efficiently.

In the kitchen
- cook with lids on pans

Boiler brainwave

If everyone in the UK with gas central heating installed a condensing boiler, we would cut carbon dioxide emissions by 18.6 million tonnes, saving £1.3 billion on our energy bills every year. This is enough energy to heat and power over 4 million homes for a year.

- use a pressure cooker
- try to keep gas flames low (if they lick up the sides of pans the gas is on too high)
- on an electric hob use flat-bottomed pans
- keep your fridge or freezer at the right temperature (3°C to 5°C for a fridge and −18°C for a freezer)
- if possible, keep your fridge away from the cooker or other sources of direct heat (e.g. direct sunlight)
- allow air to circulate behind your fridge
- defrost your freezer regularly
- don't run the tap when washing fruit and vegetables or rinsing dishes
- only run the washing machine or dishwasher with a full load
- use low-temperature washes and 'eco' settings where possible.

In the bathroom
- fix any leaky taps, toilets or water pipes
- consider installing water-saving devices in toilets and on taps or showerheads
- try replacing just one bath a week with a shower
- if you have a power shower, spend less time in it (they use as much water as baths)
- consider recycling water
- don't leave taps running when cleaning your teeth.

Lighting

Since the 1970s, electricity consumption by domestic lights and appliances has nearly doubled and is set to increase by a further 12 per cent by 2010. This rise is mainly due to the shift away from rooms lit by single-ceiling light bulbs towards multi-source lighting from wall and table lamps, as well as the fashion for multi-ceiling lights. UK households spend £1.2 billion on electricity for lighting every year, or 10 to 15 per cent of the average domestic electricity bill.

Buying energy-efficient light bulbs can cut energy wastage by over three-quarters, as they use a fraction of the energy of conventional bulbs and can last up to 10 times longer. Turning off the lights when you are not in the room or at home will also help. More information on lighting can be found in Chapter 3.

Appliances

Electrical appliances such as fridges, freezers, fridge-freezers, washing machines, tumble-driers and dishwashers consume a vast amount of energy. Every year in the UK we spend £800 million on electricity for washing machines, tumble-driers and dishwashers, and spend £1.2 billion on electricity for cooling and freezing food and drinks.

Energy-efficient appliances use less power and are cheaper to run, which means that they not only save you money, but are responsible for fewer greenhouse gas emissions at the power station. An energy-efficient washing machine uses a third of the energy of an old, inefficient model and also cuts down on water consumption.

A number of schemes and labelling systems now exist which indicate how effective electrical devices are in terms of energy usage. For example, you can look for the European Union's (EU) Energy Label or EST's blue-and-orange Energy Efficiency Recommended logo (found on anything from fridges to tumble-driers, dishwashers and light bulb packaging). The EU is slowly removing the least energy-efficient models from sale to reduce running costs and carbon dioxide emissions. See Chapter 4 for these logos and for details of the energy-efficiency schemes.

Further reading and useful websites

National Energy Action. *Energy in the Home* (3rd ed). 1996

www.dti.gov.uk/energy The Department of Trade and Industry's Energy Group

www.nea.org.uk National Energy Action

www.saveenergy.co.uk The Energy Saving Trust's consumer information website

www.ukcip.org.uk The UK Climate Impacts Programme

Chapter 2

Energy production and supply

This chapter describes the technologies of energy production: the conventional processes that currently supply the majority of our energy needs, and the alternatives that hold potential for the future. It explains how power enters our homes and how to measure the amount of energy we consume. It also provides information about 'green' electricity.

As described in Chapter 1, the world's rapidly increasing demand for energy is causing serious concern. Burning fossil fuels such as coal, petroleum oil and gas in power stations in order to generate electricity releases greenhouse gases into the atmosphere, contributing to air pollution and global climate change.

Emissions can be reduced by burning less fossil fuels and by making more use of alternative sources – such as solar power, wind power, wave power, biofuels and hydro-electric power – which do not produce (or produce significantly less) carbon dioxide. Many of these are 'renewable' and therefore have the additional benefit of reducing demand on finite fossil fuels.

Renewable energy currently contributes just 3 per cent of the UK's energy needs. However, it has the potential to supply 100 per cent of our energy. At present hydro-electric power is the predominant renewable energy in the UK, with solar and wind power set to supply the greatest proportions of our energy needs in the future.

Until recently, government support for new sources of energy has been limited – mainly because of the high costs involved in large-scale energy production. However, more money is now being made available for renewable technologies, and many schemes are becoming more economically viable. The UK government's Performance and Innovation Unit's Energy Review in February 2002 noted that renewables such as wind, wave and solar power have the potential to meet 20–30 per cent of total supply by 2020, accommodated into the national grid without major technical problems.

Under the 2002 Renewables Obligation the government set a target of increasing the proportion of electricity generated by renewable power sources. Electricity suppliers must source at least 3 per cent of their power from renewable sources in 2003, with the figure rising to 10 per cent by 2010.

The European Union has taken steps to clean up traditional power sources. In 1998 it implemented the Large Combustion Plants Directive (LCPD), which set targets for power stations, refineries and other heavy industries to reduce emissions of pollutants. In 2000 more stringent limits were agreed for new plants and existing plants were required to show a progressive reduction in emissions.

Conventional energy sources

The UK has large reserves of fossil fuels such as coal, petroleum oil and natural gas, from which the majority of our electricity output is derived. Gas is also burned directly – a process that still produces greenhouse gases, but only half as much as when converted to electricity, because energy is wasted in the conversion. Producing electricity from fossil fuels not only causes detriment to the environment but, especially in older power stations, is an inefficient process.

Between 1990 and 2000 the amount of electricity generated increased by 13 per cent. Emissions of harmful gases fell, largely caused by a gradual replacement of coal and oil with gas and nuclear power, which emit less gases when burned.

Coal

Coal was the first fossil fuel to be used to generate electricity on a large scale in the UK. The discovery of North Sea oil and gas in the 1970s offered new sources of power, although coal remains an important resource. Coal-fired power stations still account for over a third of the UK's electricity.

Power generation
Coal-burning power stations boil water to produce steam. This drives enormous turbines, which are linked to electricity generators.

A single boiler in a modern power station can burn over 260 tonnes of coal an hour. The Drax power station, in Yorkshire, is one of Europe's largest coal-fired stations.

Effect on the environment

The use of coal has various impacts on the environment. Firstly, the burning of coal in power stations releases methane, carbon dioxide, sulphur dioxide and nitrogen oxides into the atmosphere and generates contaminated water and waste products. Secondly, there is the visual effect mining activities have on the landscape. In addition, the closure of coal mines can result in derelict areas of land due to the presence of chemical waste or physical hazards such as shafts, holes and tunnels.

It has been suggested that methane gas from disused mines could be used to generate energy. Current research is, however, mainly directed towards the development of advanced combustion techniques. This would result in more electrical energy being produced by power stations, as coal would burn more cleanly and allow for the use of cheaper, lower-grade coals.

Petroleum oil

Petroluem oil plays a key role in the world's economy. It provides fuel for transport, heating and power generation and is used to make a huge range of petrochemicals and everyday products from contact lenses to camera film and CDs.

The discovery of North Sea oil in the 1970s led to the promotion of oil-fired power stations as an alternative to those burning coal. Between the late 1960s and early 1980s a significant number of large oil-fired power stations (some with coal- or gas-fired boilers on the same site) were built in the UK. The use of oil has declined in recent years, however, due to rising prices and competition from other fuels, such as gas. Nowadays, less than 10 per cent of the UK's electricity-generating capacity is made up of power stations using oil.

Power generation

Oil is burned to heat water and create steam at very high pressures. The steam then passes through the vanes of a turbine in order to drive an electricity generator. Even a relatively small 500-megawatt

27

(MW) power station may burn nearly 3,000 tonnes of heavy fuel oil in a single day. Large storage tanks are necessary to provide a uninterrupted supply.

Effect on the environment

Emissions of carbon dioxide and nitrogen oxides from oil-fired stations have fallen in recent years as a result of the reduced use of these plants. However, while oil produces less carbon dioxide and nitrogen oxides than coal for the same energy output, it creates about 20 per cent more sulphur dioxide (one of the main constituents of acid rain). There are also environmental concerns relating to the impact on the sea bed of drilling for oil and decommissioning the oil platforms.

Pollution risks of oil transportation

Power stations are normally situated either close to an oil refinery, so that oil can be piped directly, or on the coast or an estuary for deliveries by sea. However, leakages can occur at any time during exploration, production or transportation. Two major oil spills have recently occurred in our waters as a result of shipping accidents – the *Braer* in 1993 and the *Sea Empress* in 1996. The environmental impact of the *Sea Empress* running aground off the coast of South Wales was estimated to have caused the death of nearly 70,000 sea birds as well as damaging a large area of coastline supporting various eco-systems. Oil spills can also adversely affect local industries such as tourism and fishing, as has been recently witnessed off the coast of Spain.

Gas

The use of natural gas for power generation has increased rapidly since the 1990s with the removal of EU restrictions. By 2001, 28 per cent of all gas consumed in the UK was used for electricity generation. The rest is burned directly for heat, and the domestic sector accounts for about half of this. Gas is economically attractive at present and burns comparatively cleanly. In addition, a new gas-fired station can be built more quickly and cheaply than a similar one that uses oil or coal.

In recent years, gas has outstripped oil and now accounts for about 10 per cent of electricity generated, with many more plants due to come into operation. Most regional electricity companies have at least one gas-fired station. Many industrial sites have their own generating plants, often in the form of combined heat and power (CHP) installations (see page 31).

Power generation

In conventional open cycle gas turbine (OCGT) gas-fired power stations, natural gas is burned in a combustion chamber where it heats a continuous supply of compressed air. The air and burned gas expand and escape under high pressure, turning the blades of a turbine, which drives an electricity generator. The exhaust gases (which are still hot) then escape into the atmosphere, wasting much of the energy they contain.

Since 1992, combined cycle gas turbine (CCGT) power stations have included a second stage, which uses residual heat to generate more electricity. They can convert more than half the chemical energy of the gas to electrical energy. This compares favourably with any other kind of fossil-fuel power station (except combined heat and power plants – see page 31).

Effect on the environment

As gas burns relatively cleanly, the government is encouraging its use to help achieve national targets for reducing total emissions of pollutants (see Chapter 1). Although carbon dioxide is a by-product, the newer power stations burn much less fuel per unit of electricity generated than coal- or oil-fired stations. The result is less carbon dioxide emissions – only half that emitted by coal-fired stations. In addition, natural gas produces very little sulphur dioxide and emits only about a quarter as much nitrogen oxides as coal per unit of electricity generated.

Since gas is extracted at the same point as oil, many of the environmental issues – such as the impact of drilling and decommissioning – are the same. Gas flaring, subject to strict government regulation, is a process which is used offshore to separate gas from oil. When gas is flared, emissions of carbon dioxide, methane and nitrous oxide are released into the environment.

Losses can occur during the transmission and distribution of gas, which results in the release of methane into the atmosphere. In

2000 around 330,000 tonnes of methane were released into the atmosphere as a result of gas leakage, representing 15 per cent of all methane emissions. As a contributor to climate change, methane is second only to carbon dioxide.

Nuclear power

Nuclear power currently provides 26 per cent of all Britain's electricity. This contrasts with more widespread usage in other European countries such as France (75 per cent), Sweden (45 per cent) and Germany (30 per cent).

Britain's nuclear power stations have output capacities similar to their coal- and oil-fired counterparts – from about 200–500 MW for the older reactors, up to well over 1,000 MW for the newer, advanced gas-cooled reactors (AGR) and pressurised water reactors (PWR). Sizewell is the UK's only PWR.

Power generation

Nuclear power stations use uranium to generate electricity. One tonne of uranium can produce as much electricity as 2,000 tonnes of coal and, once it has been used, it can be reprocessed and recycled to make more fuel. During the reprocessing, plutonium is given off as a by-product which, in turn, can then be used to generate power in fast reactors.

Effect on the environment

Unlike fossil-fuel stations, nuclear power stations produce virtually no carbon dioxide. They also emit hardly any sulphur dioxide or nitrogen oxides, and so do not contribute to acid rain or global warming. Worldwide reserves of uranium could last hundreds of times longer than all fossil fuels combined. Nuclear power is a reliable way of maintaining electrical production if other fuel sources are interrupted or as top-up during high demand. Using nuclear power also reduces the rate at which we use up the limited world resources of coal, gas and oil.

However, critics of nuclear power voice concerns over the dangers of radioactive emissions, the risk of accidents and the long-term effects of the disposal and storage of waste. This is a serious drawback to nuclear power as the waste generated by the nuclear industry is radioactive and poses a threat to human health and the environment. It needs to be disposed of with extreme care. There are three classifications of radioactive waste.

- **High-level waste** is made up of material separated from uranium and plutonium during reprocessing. This is very radioactive and must therefore be stored in large steel tanks, or made into solid blocks of glass in a process called vitrification.
- **Intermediate-level waste** is made up of contaminated equipment and sludges from various treatment processes.
- **Low-level waste** is items such as clothing and laboratory equipment which may have come into contact with radioactive materials. This waste has a small radioactive content and is generally disposed of deep underground.

Safety concerns have also been expressed about nuclear power stations which have reached the end of their useful life. These are 'decommissioned', which means dismantling them and removing their radioactive fuel and coolant. Three British stations are currently undergoing decommissioning – a process that can take several years.

The view of Consumers' Association is that the issue of waste disposal must be satisfactorily resolved, and that it would be irresponsible and unwise to start down the route of new nuclear build until a means of disposing of existing high and intermediate level waste is found – one that commands widespread public support and does not require continuous monitoring for the foreseeable future. Meanwhile, government should maintain a 'neutral stance' towards nuclear power.

Combined heat and power (CHP) stations

During electricity generation a large amount of low-grade heat is produced as a by-product which, in conventional power stations, is lost. In combined heat and power (CHP) systems, this heat can be recycled, with as much as 80 per cent of the fuel's chemical energy being converted into electricity and useful heat.

CHPs are highly efficient and can be designed for any type of fuel although gas is the most popular for industrial purposes. At the time of writing, about 1,400 CHP systems exist in the UK, providing about 4 per cent of the UK's total electricity output. There are environmental benefits to CHPs, as the plants produce

31

30 per cent less carbon emissions than coal-fired stations and 10 per cent less than gas-fired power stations. They also produce lower emissions of sulphur dioxide and nitrogen oxides, helping to reduce acid rain.

Renewable energy sources

Unlike fossil fuels, most renewable energy sources do not release carbon dioxide as a by-product into the atmosphere. Those that do, such as biomass, are 'carbon neutral'. In other words, they absorb the same amount of carbon dioxide from the atmosphere during their growth as is generated when they are burned. Examples of renewable resources include:

- wind power
- solar power
- biofuels
- hydro-electric power (HEP)
- geothermal energy
- tidal power
- wave power.

Wind power

Wind power has enormous potential as a renewable source of energy. Despite some promising initiatives, wind-generated energy still accounts for less than 1 per cent of Britain's total electricity output. This should rise, however, as many new wind schemes are being built each year.

Many countries are already demonstrating their commitment to wind power, and some – notably the USA – have invested heavily in further developing this technology.

In addition to those used for large-scale energy production, wind turbines of a size suitable for domestic use are available (see Chapter 8).

Power generation
The most common type of wind turbine has blades mounted on a horizontal shaft like an aircraft propeller. The shaft drives an electrical generator through a step-up gearbox, and the whole assembly

can be turned to face the wind direction. In more advanced machines, the blade angle can be adjusted according to wind speed to regulate the rotation rate for maximum efficiency. In an alternative design, the drive shaft is positioned vertically with a horizontally spinning rotor. More power is created if you have bigger blades or higher wind speeds.

Some very large machines have been built – for example, one in the Orkney Islands has a tower 45 metres high and a two-blade turbine 60 metres across from tip to tip, with a gearbox and generator unit weighing over 100 tonnes. Its peak output is three megawatts (MW). However, the enormous cyclical stresses in such large machines tend to cause mechanical problems.

Most commercial generation schemes are based on medium-sized turbines with outputs of around 300 to 700 kilowatts (kW), arranged in groups known as wind farms. In the UK a wind farm typically has 10 to 20 machines. Smaller schemes need some form of back-up, such as solar or diesel generators, if used to supply remote, non-grid-connected applications.

Effect on the environment

In contrast to fossil fuels, wind power is a non-polluting source of energy, although wind variability, which limits wind power's contribution to national supplies, is still a drawback. Somewhat more controversial is the fact that wind farms are highly visible and can be noisy – although offshore wind farms offer a solution to this problem.

Winds of change

The government has made wind power a key element of its new national targets for encouraging renewable sources (see Chapter 1) and major commercial generators such as Powergen and Scottish Power, as well as several regional electricity companies, are already involved in wind farm projects.

Solar power

The sun gives out vast amounts of energy, mostly in the form of electromagnetic waves, which range from infrared through visible light to ultraviolet. About half this energy is reflected back into space or absorbed by the Earth's atmosphere. The remaining solar energy is still potentially sufficient to supply our needs, if only we could find a way to capture and convert it efficiently.

Solar energy can be utilised in one of three main ways:

- by trapping it after it has passed through glass (passive solar heating)
- by heating water in a solar collector
- by converting it to electricity in a solar cell (photovoltaics).

Solar energy can make an effective contribution to hot-water heating but – apart from 'passive' solar heating (see below) – as yet nobody has found a way to utilise solar power effectively for space heating. To do this would mean storing the heat for several months, since most solar energy in the UK arrives in the summer and space heating is needed in the winter. For solar energy to reach its full potential and solar cells to be incorporated into new or existing buildings, their cost will have to come down, as they are still relatively expensive.

Passive solar heating

Solar energy can be used to heat buildings directly, using the 'green-house' principle. This simply means direct sunlight entering a room and warming the interior, which re-radiates energy but only at longer wavelengths (infrared) – which cannot pass back through the glass. In other words, the heat is trapped inside the room. Double glazing reduces heat loss to the air outside, and heat efficiency can be increased if there is a black-painted wall behind the glass to absorb and store the incoming heat energy.

To be effective, passive solar technology means designing buildings with large, south-facing windows and small windows facing north. This ensures that the building receives the maximum possible sunlight and loses the least amount of heat. On a small scale, you can employ passive solar heating by opening the curtains during the day to allow heat gain, and closing them at dusk to keep warm air in.

For more details, see Chapter 8.

Solar collectors

Solar-heated hot water systems are the most common applications of solar energy in the UK. They use the sun's warmth to heat water as it passes through a solar collector, which is angled to receive the maximum amount of solar radiation. Combined with a well-insulated storage cylinder, a solar collector can provide a substantial proportion of the hot water a family needs. You can buy solar collectors for home use, or build DIY versions. For examples of this technology in a domestic setting, see Chapter 8.

Solar cells

More commonly referred to as photovoltaic cells, these are small devices made from crystalline semiconductors – similar to those used in computer chips and control panel indicator lights. The output of a single cell is less than 1 volt and can supply only a very small current. Fortunately, cells can be connected together in series to give higher voltages and in parallel to provide more current.

One square metre of solar cells can generate about 100 watts at midday in summer and about 10 watts on average throughout the year. Large arrays of cells assembled in panels can supply hundreds or even thousands of watts. At present, solar-cell panels are too expensive for everyday energy uses. They are typically used with a back-up battery to power remote equipment such as climate monitoring stations and telecommunications relays. On a much smaller scale, they are used for powering low-wattage equipment, such as battery chargers, lights and pumps.

Significantly cheaper solar cells, based on amorphous silicon and other thin-film semiconductors, are now being developed. If costs come down sufficiently, solar cells could be incorporated into cladding for the outer walls of buildings or in window glass. Solar tiles are now available, and some liquid solar cells are being developed which can store charge like a battery, to provide power even at night. Developments such as these could soon transform the economics and practicability of solar panels. See Chapter 8 for examples of these technologies in use.

Solar power stations

Non-polluting solar power stations provide electricity economically in locations with more sunshine than the UK. The main requirement is plenty of land area. For example, to replace a relatively small fossil-fuel power station with a generating capacity of, say, 200MW would require an area of more than a square kilometre.

The two successful types of solar power station both use the sun's heat to boil water, creating steam, which drives a conventional turbine electricity generator. The 'power tower' uses hundreds of steerable mirrors, which continuously track the sun, focusing its heat on to a high-temperature boiler at the top of the tower. Power towers with 1MW capacities have been built in Sicily and the French Pyrenees, while a 10MW tower is operating in Southern California.

The 'solar field' method consists of many long, trough-shaped parabolic mirrors side by side. Pipes run along the focus of each of these mirrors, carrying a fluid that transfers the heat to a boiler to raise steam. One of the world's largest solar-power projects, in the Mojave Desert of California, has several solar fields which each cover about 200,000 square metres and produce 30MW of electrical power.

Biofuels

These are a range of renewable fuels, derived from organic sources. Although they emit carbon dixoxide when burned, they are 'carbon neutral' (i.e. they absorb an equivalent amount of carbon dioxide from the atmosphere during their growth). They can take the solid form of biomass or that of biogas.

Biomass

Biomass is a general name for waste material derived from plants or from animal manure which can be burned, either to produce electricity or as solid fuel for heat. Refuse-derived fuel (RDF) is made up mainly of plant material and may be used raw or highly processed in the form of pellets. Cereal and other crops such as rape-seed can also be cultivated as biomass fuel. Another promising source is coppiced wood, taken from fast-growing trees on wasteland or from diversified farmland, which is harvested on a three- to five-year cycle. The wood is then chipped to burn more efficiently.

There are several RDF power stations in the UK. Two demonstration power stations use poultry litter to generate electricity. Using biomass in this way is still experimental and provides only 0.25 per cent of the UK's total electricity generating capacity.

Solid fuel as a direct source of heating is an alternative to gas or electricity. When run efficiently these systems (wood-fuel, for example) do not produce much in the way of smoke emissions. See Chapter 3 for more about heating systems.

Biogas

Biogas is produced when organic materials such as sewage, animal manure and organic household and industrial waste decompose in a situation where little or no air is present. As biogas consists of approximately two-thirds methane and one-third carbon dioxide, it burns well and can be used to provide heat or electrical energy.

Like biomass, biogas technology is relatively experimental and currently accounts for about 0.6 per cent of the UK's total electricity output. However, some regional electricity companies are already operating biogas stations and combined heat and power (CHP) schemes which serve local communities.

Power generation

Biomass is used to generate power in a similar way to fossil fuels, by burning it in a furnace to heat water and produce steam. Although most biomass power stations are fairly small and simple, CHP systems (see page 31) can improve the efficiency by utilising waste heat which would normally be lost.

Energy can also be extracted from biomass by fermentation or pyrolysis (heating without air). This creates fuels such as ethanol and methanol or methane gas which can then be used to generate electricity, or for transport.

Biogas can be collected as a by-product from landfill sites when the organic matter starts to decompose. If the waste is covered with a layer of clay, the gas is prevented from escaping and can be extracted at a controlled rate.

Biogas is also extracted from sewage. At a sewage works the raw sewage is screened, then pumped into sedimentation tanks where the solid organic matter settles as sludge. The sludge is pumped into huge anaerobic digester tanks, where it spends about seven weeks at a temperature of 26°C to 28°C. Over this period about half the organic matter is converted into gas.

Effect on the environment

Biomass and biogas can reduce the problem of waste disposal, and the former often makes use of redundant or poor-quality farmland. Landfill sites are a significant source of biogas, but opinion is divided as to whether these provide the best solution to waste disposal.

Burning biomass and biogas releases pollutants, albeit in small quantities, which would be a factor to consider if their use increased.

Hydro-electric power (HEP)

The term hydro-electric power is normally applied to electrical power generated from inland water such as streams, rivers and lakes.

In the UK, hydro-electric (hydro) power stations have been in operation since the mid-1960s and range from small 30kW generators to those with outputs over 100MW – comparable with a gas turbine or small coal-fired station. However, as most of the suitable sites have already been utilised, there are no plans to develop any more large-scale hydro schemes in the UK.

The largest British hydro-electric power stations, at Ffestiniog and Dinorwig in Wales, and Cruachan and Foyers in Scotland, have output capacities in the 300–400MW range. The Dinorwig station has a generating capacity of over 1.7 thousand MW (1.7GW) – greater than any of our nuclear power stations and equivalent to the largest coal-fired stations. Between them, these four schemes can provide up to 4 per cent of the UK's electricity demand during peak periods. On average, hydro schemes generate about 2 per cent of our electricity.

Power generation

Water is fed through pipes at a controlled rate from a high reservoir to an electricity generating station lower down. In the station the high-pressure flow of water causes turbines to spin, driving electric generators. The most efficient turbines can convert up to 90 per cent of the water's energy into electricity.

In a pumped storage hydro station, the turbines can also be used in reverse to pump water up from the lower reservoir to replenish the upper reservoir. Pumped storage schemes can start generating in as little as 10 seconds to meet a surge in demand. They can be very unobtrusive since they use natural lakes as reservoirs, while the generating station may be hidden in a chamber excavated from the mountains.

Effect on the environment

Unlike fossil-fuel power stations, hydro-electric power emits no pollutants, but as with any large-scale development a large hydro scheme will have an adverse effect on the surrounding environment. Large hydro schemes around the globe have been cited as having a major impact on river flow, and the elimination of seasonal flooding which is essential for depositing fertile silts on surrounding farmland. This, in turn, has resulted in the displacement of native communities living in newly flooded areas near the scheme.

Geothermal energy

Geothermal energy from beneath the Earth's surface, found in naturally hot water, steam or dry rocks, can be harnessed to generate electricity. This is not generally considered to be a renewable energy source, because removing large amounts of heat can lower the natural temperature of extraction sites, which must then be abandoned until they recover. This may take many years.

Using geothermal energy to generate electricity is currently a very expensive process, unless, as in the hot springs of New Zealand, the heat is readily accessible near the surface. New Zealand is able to provide about 30 per cent of the country's electricity using geothermal energy, but other countries have failed to reach an output of one per cent.

Power generation

All current extraction methods involve the flow of hot fluids to the surface. Boreholes are required to obtain heat energy from underground sources. Water pumped through rocks may be converted to steam or run through a heat exchanger, while steam can be used to generate electricity if directed through turbines.

> **Hot stuff in Hampshire**
>
> In aquifers (porous rocks such as limestone and sandstone about 2km beneath the Earth's surface), the water temperature may reach 100°C or more. High pressure underground prevents the water from turning to steam, but at the surface it can be released to drive a steam turbine linked to an electricity generator. A district heating system in Southampton uses aquifer water to provide energy.

Effect on the environment

Geothermal energy does not release carbon dioxide or pollutants. However, in urban areas borehole drilling could be a short-term nuisance. The sulphurous smell of hot aquifers may cause problems, and there is a risk of radioactive gases such as radon rising in boreholes. Engineers would also need to consider any possible effects on the local geology, such as subsidence or slippage, in unstable regions.

Tidal power

Two-thirds of the Earth's surface is covered by sea. This huge body of water experiences strong gravitational forces from the moon and sun, which cause tides – the regular rise and fall in sea level. In suitable locations, this movement can be used to generate electricity.

Normally, tidal power schemes are built across the mouth of a river estuary or coastal bay as they need a large storage basin in order to be effective.

Despite an extensive coastline, which offers great potential to exploit the use of tidal power, the UK currently has no tidal schemes in operation. In France, a tidal barrage across the estuary of the River Rance in Brittany has been generating electricity since 1966. Its output capacity is 240MW – broadly comparable with a small coal-fired power station. Smaller tidal schemes have been built in Russia, China and Canada.

Tidal ranges (the difference in height between low and high tide) vary greatly from place to place because of the effects of local geography. The average around the world is about 1m, but some locations experience tidal ranges that are much greater. The most suitable ranges for power generation are generally between five and ten metres.

Tidal ranges along the west coast of England and Wales are unusually large, averaging 7–8m on the spring tides in several estuaries and as much as 11 metres in the Severn. The Severn estuary is the site for the most ambitious tidal barrage that has been proposed for the UK so far. It could supply about six per cent of our present electricity requirements. Other major proposals include barrages across the Mersey, Dee, Humber and Thames estuaries as well as Morecambe Bay, the Solway Firth and the Wash.

Tidal schemes have major advantages. The energy source is renewable, reliable and completely predictable. A barrage may give useful protection against tidal surges and flooding, and provide other benefits such as a new road crossing and recreational facilities – in turn stimulating local development.

The main obstacle to exploiting tidal power is the cost. The Severn barrage would cost about £11 billion and take as much as nine years to build. There are also environmental concerns (see below).

Power generation

Tubular ducts in the barrage contain huge turbines, which drive electricity generators. Sluice gates are opened to allow each incoming 'flood' tide to fill the estuary basin. At high tide the sluice gates are closed, then opened on the 'ebb' tide as the sea level outside falls. Water from the basin escapes through the ducts, spinning the turbines to generate electricity. However, this arrangement only generates power during ebb tides.

The barrage across the Rance estuary in Brittany has reversible turbines, which can generate power on flood tides as well. They can also be used as pumps to increase high-tide water levels above their natural level. It makes sense to do this if a high tide coincides with a period of low electricity demand. By topping up the water level with cheap off-peak electricity, the barrage can be used to supply more electricity during the next period of heavy demand.

Effect on the environment

Although tidal power stations emit no atmospheric pollutants, building a barrage across a large estuary or bay can cause changes to tidal heights and have a detrimental effect on the nature of mudflats and sandbanks. This means that local plant and animal populations, who depend on tidal mudflats for food, are adversely affected.

Wave power

Waves around the UK are some of the most energetic in the world. In some locations every metre of wave-front contains an average 50kW of power, which would be sufficient to supply several homes with electricity if it could be efficiently captured and converted.

Although tapping a small proportion of the available wave energy could make a significant contribution to our electricity supply, the technology to do this is still at an early stage of development.

Power generation

If they proved successful, wave-power devices would be clustered together in 'energy farms' floating several kilometres from the shore. The reason for locating them at this distance is that they need to be in deep water (waves lose energy as they approach the shore). Farms would be linked to the national grid by undersea cables.

Effect on the environment

Once operating, a wave-power station would be virtually pollution free. Shore-based stations – considered unsuitable for generating electricity on a large scale – could supply local needs in remote locations such as islands. If carefully designed, these could be fairly small and unobtrusive. By contrast, offshore wave energy farms would occupy large areas of sea. They would be sited far out enough so as not to be unsightly from the land, but since they would pose a potential hazard to shipping, they would require extensive warning systems.

How power reaches your home

Gas

Currently, approximately 80 per cent of households have access to a mains gas supply, with most of our gas coming from beneath the North Sea and Irish Sea, and from the Interconnector – a pipeline that links the UK to the European gas network. Major companies, including many in the oil sector, also pipe gas from offshore production platforms. Almost all pipelines are owned and operated by National Grid Transco*, formerly part of British Gas, which is regulated by the Office of Gas and Electricity Markets (OFGEM)*.

Gas producers compete with one another to sell gas to gas shippers (traders who arrange for the gas to be transported to a gas supply company).

The company that supplies your home with gas will send you a bill for the amount of gas you use and for the services it provides such as reading the meter, handling your account and sending you the bill. Your bill will also include charges for the cost of gas, storage and transportation.

Electricity

Most of our electricity is supplied as alternating current (AC) through the National Grid. Electricity can also be imported and exported through direct current (DC) links with Scotland and France. The remainder is generated privately, with a small contribution in the form of low-voltage electricity from batteries or solar cells.

Since the market was privatised in 1999, different structures have been created for England and Wales, Scotland and Northern Ireland. In England and Wales the virtual monopoly on transmission and distribution is separated from those areas of the business which are based on competition.

Electricity is transmitted throughout England and Wales by National Grid Transco* and is distributed locally to consumers by regional electricity companies. Scotland has three private electricity companies who operate their own generation, transmission and distribution networks: Scottish Power, British Energy and Scottish and Southern Energy. Northern Ireland has three public generating companies which sell their output to Northern Ireland Electricity for transmission, distribution and supply.

The generating companies sell their electricity to suppliers through a trading system known as the Electricity Pool, in which the market price is set every half-hour of the day and varies according to demand and availability. OFGEM (see 'Gas', above) regulates the price of distribution.

Electricity travels from the generators that create it, first along high-voltage transmission lines and then through a lower-voltage local distribution system. Transformers then reduce the voltage to 240v for household use.

A mixture of overhead lines and underground cables are used. In general, overhead lines carry electricity in rural areas and underground lines carry electricity in urban areas. Only three per cent of electricity is carried on pylons, which are used for the highest voltages on the network.

In the same way as a gas supplier, the company that provides your home with electricity will send you a bill for the amount you use and for services such as administration and reading the meter. Your bill also includes charges for generation, transmission, distribution and a small contribution to the Renewables Obligation (see page 12), which helps fund renewable electricity projects. In addition, every customer pays on average £1.20 per year to fund energy-efficiency measures.

Protection for consumers

Energywatch* is an independent gas and electricity consumer watchdog. It is the first port of call for customers in Britain who have not been able to resolve complaints with gas or electricity companies. Energywatch also provides information on changing supplier (see 'Cutting the cost of your bills', page 51) and on gas and electricity safety.

The Office of Gas and Electricity Markets (OFGEM)* regulates the gas and electricity industries in the UK. Its primary function is to protect the interests of consumers by promoting competition, but it also has a duty to take account of the interests of pensioners, disabled people, those suffering chronic illness, people on low incomes and those living in rural areas.

'Green' electricity

The Renewables Obligation requires electricity suppliers to provide a growing proportion of energy from renewable sources (see page 12). 'Green' electricity is generated from renewable sources such as wind power, hydro-electric power, solar power and biofuels, but is delivered through the National Grid in the same way that conventional electricity is delivered.

As green energy uses the same cables, grids and meters as conventional electricity, you do not need to have special equipment installed. To switch to a green tariff, simply obtain a form from one of the suppliers listed in Appendix I at the back of this book. All that they will require from you is a meter reading on the switchover date. For information on how to do this see 'Measuring and calculating fuel consumption', overleaf. For advice about switching your energy supplier, see www.switchwithwhich.co.uk.

Signing up to a green tariff does not guarantee that you will receive green electricity, but it does mean that somewhere on the grid your demand for electricity is being matched by the equivalent supply of green electricity. This means that your supplier needs to produce, or buy from a producer, an amount of power from renewable sources equivalent to your consumption.

For each unit of electricity they buy or produce, suppliers receive Renewables Obligation Certificates (ROCs), which must be submitted to OFGEM each year to prove that they have reached the required proportion of green electricity. Suppliers that fail to meet the legal target can buy more ROCs from suppliers willing to trade, or pay a buy-out price to OFGEM. This is redistributed to companies that meet the target to reward them for their compliance.

Types of tariff

Currently you can choose from two types of green energy product: energy-based tariffs and fund-based tariffs. With an energy-based tariff, you receive a commitment from the supplier that your electricity consumption will be matched with the same amount of green electricity. With a fund-based tariff, you continue to receive conventional electricity, but contributions are deducted from your bill – either at a fixed rate or in the form of a premium. Suppliers may match your contribution or make separate donations. The funds can then be used for building renewable energy plants, providing grants for community renewable projects, promoting energy efficiency measures, raising awareness of environmental problems in schools and other institutions, or for wildlife conservation. Different types of funds are administered differently and you should contact your chosen supplier directly for details.

Many combination products exist. In this case, the supplier matches your demand for electricity with renewable supply and you also make contributions to a fund. These are the most common type of green tariff available.

Suppliers in Britain (with the exception of Seeboard, which is solely fund-based) must make clear to customers how their tariff meets the legal requirements of the Renewables Obligation, and explain any environmental benefits it offers.

Green tariffs are normally more expensive than conventional electricity tariffs, so it is still worth trying to cut down on the energy you use in the home.

To help consumers compare information about products that are currently available, Friends of the Earth (FOE)★ has produced a league table of green tariffs – contact the organisation for details.

Appendix I at the back of this book details some of the green electricity deals offered by suppliers at the time of writing.

Measuring and calculating fuel consumption

You can work out roughly what your weekly or monthly fuel costs might be by keeping a record of the fuel intake to your home. The easiest way to do this is to keep an eye on your electricity and gas meters, as this will help keep track of periods of high fuel consumption, such as in winter months.

The following units are used for different types of fuel.

- Gas is measured in cubic feet.
- Electricity is measured in kilowatt hours (kWh).
- Coal is measured in kilograms or tonnes.
- Bottled gas and oil are measured in litres (or gallons).

For the purposes of determining energy efficiency, these different measurements can be confusing because it is difficult to compare them. Heat energy can be measured in a number of ways – for example, in megajoules per cubic foot for gas or in kilowatt hours for electricity. See 'Calculating gas consumption', page 50, for a rough conversion rate between gas and electricity units.

Electricity ratings

The watt (W) and kilowatt (1 kW = 1,000 watts) signify the rate at which energy is used. So a 100W light bulb will use power at a faster rate than a 60W bulb over the same period. The watt hour (Wh) or kilowatt hour (kWh) is the amount of energy used.

All electrical appliances carry a 'wattage' rating (also showing the voltage frequency, for AC devices, and the maximum current requirement), which should be clearly marked on the appliance itself. The power required by household appliances varies over a wide range, from about 5W for an electric door bell to ratings approaching 1,000W for appliances with motors (such as mixers) and up to 20,000W (20kW) for a large electric heating system. Heating appliances use the most power and have ratings from 1kW to 20kW (although any device over 3kW must not be plugged into a normal plug socket).

Calculating electricity consumption

You can roughly calculate the amount of energy used by an electric appliance by looking at its power rating (wattage) and the length of time for which you use it. You can work out the cost of the power used by looking at the cost per unit of electricity, which will be shown on your electricity bill. So:

Rating in kilowatts × time in hours = amount of electricity used in kWh

KWh × cost per unit = cost of electricity used

If the wattage is expressed in watts, rather than kilowatts, divide by 1,000. If the time is measured in hours, rather than minutes, divide by 60. So:

Rating in watts ÷ 1,000 × time in minutes ÷ 60 = amount of electricity used in kWh

Example 1

An immersion heater rated at 3kW takes four hours to heat the hot water tank from cold. The electricity charge rate shown on the quarterly bill is 7.5p per unit (1 unit = 1kWh).

So the electric energy used to heat the water is 4 hours $\times$ 3kW = 12kWh (12 units of electricity).

The cost of heating the water is 12 $\times$ the charge rate per unit = 12 $\times$ 7.5p = 90p.

Example 2

A dishwasher is used twice a day. The wash cycle lasts 1.5 hours. The electric power required for the wash cycle averages 2kW. The electricity charge rate is the same as above (7.5p per unit).

So the electric energy used per wash cycle is 1.5 hours $\times$ 2kW = 3kWh (3 units of electricity).

The electric energy used daily for dishwashing = number of wash cycles $\times$ energy used per cycle = 2 $\times$ 3kWh = 6kWh (6 units of electricity).

The daily cost of using the dishwasher = 6$\times$ the charge rate per unit = 6 $\times$ 7.5p = 45p.

Note that this method of calculation does not take into account the effect of thermostats or timers turning appliances on or off. You should factor in the times when devices are switched off.

Reading an electricity meter

There are three types of electricity meter:

- digital meters
- dial meters
- Economy 7 meters.

All types of meter display the number of units of electricity used. (One unit of electricity is a kilowatt hour – see page 47.)

To measure your use of electricity over a set period (days or weeks) you need to take a reading at the beginning and end of that period of time. The difference between the two is the number of units of electricity you have consumed.

Digital meters

These meters have a row of numbers that show the quantity of electricity consumed. The last number, ringed in red, shows 'tenths of a unit'. Ignore this number. Read the first five numbers from the left to right.

Dial meters

These older meters have a row of clock-like dials ranging from 0 to 9. Starting with the dial on the far left, write down the numbers the hands point to. Ignore 'tenth of a unit'. Always take the number that the hand has gone past, and not the one it is closest to. If the hand is almost directly over a number, the reading is that number; if it has not quite reached it, the reading is the previous number.

Economy 7 meters

On Economy 7 tariff (or White Meter in Scotland), all electricity used during the night is charged at a cheaper rate. These meters have two rows of numbers, one marked 'normal' (for on-peak or daytime hours), the other marked 'low' (for off-peak or night-time hours).

A small pointer indicates whether the supply currently registered is off-peak or on-peak electricity. You should take both 'low' and 'normal' readings and record them separately. You can add them together to tell you how much electricity you have used in total.

To calculate how much your electricity has cost you in a given period, multiply the separate readings by the cost per unit for each charge rate, as follows.

The cost of on-peak electricity = (new reading 'normal' minus old reading 'normal') × normal unit charge.

The cost of off-peak electricity = (new reading 'low' minus old reading 'low') × off-peak unit charge.

Add these together to find the total cost.

Calculating gas consumption

Although the units of gas measurement are cubic feet, gas charges are based on units of gas used. What this unit is will depend on your meter: it may be 100 cubic feet, or, on a metric meter, 1 cubic metre. The cost per unit of gas will be stated on your bill. So to find out the cost of gas used over a given period you need to read the meter to find the number of units used (see 'Reading a gas meter' below), and multiply this by the cost per unit as shown on your bill.

In order to make a comparison between the energy used in gas and that used in electricity, you will need to convert the gas units to kWh. As a general calculating rule, each unit of gas is the equivalent of 32kWh of energy. So to calculate the total energy value of the gas you should multiply the number of gas units by 32.

In fact, most gas bills, in addition to showing the total gas used in units, now convert these to kWh.

Reading a gas meter

There are two types of gas meter: digital and dial varieties. Whichever sort you have, to measure your gas use over a period of days or weeks, take meter readings at the beginning and end of that period. The difference between the two readings tells you how many units have been used.

Digital meters
The white numbers show the units (hundreds of cubic feet) you have used. The red number to the right is tens of cubic feet. Ignore this number and read only the first four numbers from left to right.

Dial meters
Gas dial meters work the same way as electric dial meters (see previous page) but the arrangement of dials is slightly different. Read four dials from left to right, recording the number that the pointer has gone past. Do not record the dial that says '100 per rev' or the large dial.

Readings if you have a prepayment meter
If you pay for gas or electricity with a prepayment meter, you should still have a meter which registers fuel consumption. Taking a reading from this meter is a more accurate way of recording fuel

consumption than measuring the units of fuel used, as the total cost will include an amount to cover standing charges and possibly also a contribution towards the repayment of any debts.

Cutting the cost of your bills

Thanks to privatisation in 1998 and 1999, consumers can now choose which company to buy their gas and electricity from.

The size of your gas or electricity bill ultimately depends on how much you use but, because different companies' tariffs work in different ways, it's not always straightforward which will be the cheapest. For example, a company with a high standing charge (the amount you pay each month, regardless of how much you use) might have a low tariff (rate per unit used). This might be a good deal for a large family which uses a lot of gas or electricity. On the other hand, a company with a small standing charge, but a higher tariff may work out cheaper for a person living alone, who only uses small amounts.

To work out which companies offer the best deal, you need to do the following calculation:

- Add up your gas or electricity usage in kWh (kilowatt hours) from last year's quarterly bills.
- Calculate the gas/electricity costs by multiplying the company's unit rate (pence per kWh) by the amount you use.
- Add on the annual standing charge.

Some websites can help do the calculations for you. There are now seven companies signed up to Energywatch's code of practice for price-comparison websites – listed below. You could also try www.greenprices.co.uk, for green suppliers. Simply key in your details and they will come up with your likely bills from all the gas and electricity suppliers in your area.

www.blays.co.uk/energy   www.ukpower.co.uk
www.buy.co.uk   www.unravelit.com
www.saveonyourbills.co.uk   www.uswitch.com
www.theenergyshop.com

Alternatively, you can contact Energywatch* for a series of fact-sheets with all the companies' tariffs.

Smart metering

All gas companies and all but a few electricity companies are legally required to supply energy through an appropriate meter. In 2001 the government set up a Smart Metering Working Group to consider how new technology might save energy, cut people's bills, manage demand and reduce emissions. It calculated that meters which are easier to read and provide more accurate information could reduce domestic fuel bills by an annual average of £24. Some new Internet meters have built-in modems and can communicate with other devices in the home. However, the cost to consumers and a lack of standardisation have so far prevented smart meters becoming widespread.

Useful websites

www.dti.gov.uk/energy The Department of Trade and Industry's Energy Group

www.energywatch.org.uk The independent gas and electricity consumer watchdog

www.switchwithwhich.co.uk For advice on changing your energy supplier

Chapter 3

Saving energy

Conserving energy, whatever its source, has a positive effect on both the environment and the size of our household bills. The ways in which we heat, light and insulate our homes play a significant part in successful energy saving. This chapter suggests practical measures you can take to improve the energy efficiency of yours.

Over half the energy we use in our homes is for heating rooms and water. It is therefore crucial to get the most out of your heating and hot water systems in order to minimise energy wastage. Slowing down the rate at which heat escapes from your home is also important. This can be accomplished by some straightforward DIY insulation measures.

When you consider undertaking energy-saving measures in your home, it is important to assess how worthwhile they will be in terms of energy saved, and also how long it will be before you start seeing a return on your money. For some measures, such as lagging a hot-water cylinder, this will be quite short, while for others (such as wall insulation) it could be many years before the initial cost is defrayed.

A number of grants and schemes are available to help pay for energy-efficiency improvements. Some also give advice on energy-efficient lighting. A number of those available at the time of writing are listed in Appendix II at the back of this book.

Insulation and draught-proofing

Heat moves from the hotter areas of a building to cooler ones, then is lost to the outside or to the parts of the building that are not in use. This happens in two ways: through fabric heat loss (via the parts of a building that are exposed either to the outside or to some other

53

unheated space), and through ventilation heat loss (as a result of air flow into and out of the building). The more you can slow down the rate at which this happens, the less heat you need to generate. You can reduce fabric heat loss through insulation, and ventilation heat loss through draught-proofing.

Insulation is the most important of all energy-saving measures because it can have the greatest effect on our energy expenditure. Most of the heat lost from our homes goes directly through the walls, roof, windows and floors. Insulating the average home can reduce the amount of heat lost in this way by at least half. As well as saving you money on your fuel bills, insulating also makes a house more comfortable, as it creates a more even temperature throughout the home.

Draught-proofing is one of the easiest and cheapest energy-saving measures. This stops air getting into or out of the home in an uncontrolled way. Draughts can account for anything from 10 to 30 per cent of a household's total energy expenditure – the national total would translate into thousands of tons of carbon dioxide emissions caused by generating wasted power. Your house does, however, need a constant supply of fresh air – for you to breathe, for certain fuel-burning appliances to work properly and safely, and to prevent condensation. Controlled ventilation ensures that sufficient fresh air gets in and that odours and moisture-laden air are removed.

The following pages outline some basic measures for reducing heat loss around the house, including draught-proofing and insulating hot water pipes and cylinders, lofts, external walls, windows and floors. Some are very simple DIY techniques; others are more complicated and will involve calling in the professionals.

Building materials

The different materials that are used in the exterior of a building – for example, brick, wood, glass or concrete – each allow heat to pass through them at a different rate. Depending on the types of material and their thickness, some parts of the building will be more effective than others at keeping the heat inside.

The standard measure of the rate of heat flow through material is known as the 'U-value'. In technical terms, a U-value is a measure of the rate (in watts) at which heat will flow through each square

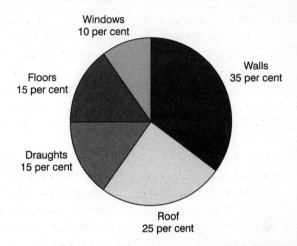

Heat loss in an uninsulated home

The chart shows the amount of heat lost in different areas of a house without any insulation.

Windows
10 per cent

Floors
15 per cent

Walls
35 per cent

Draughts
15 per cent

Roof
25 per cent

Because your home is probably at least partly insulated, the heat loss from different parts is unlikely to correspond exactly to the figures above. However, the chart does indicate which areas it is most important to insulate.

metre of any given material, for each 1°C difference between the inside and outside temperatures. The lower the U-value, the slower the rate at which heat will escape. Single-glazed windows have quite a high rate of heat loss because window glass is very thin and is a good conductor of heat.

In order to meet the requirements of the latest Building Regulations (see box overleaf), U-values have to be lower than certain maximum amounts. The following U-values are the maximum likely to meet the regulations:

Roofs   0.16–0.25 (depending on where insulation is)

Floors   0.25

Windows and   2–2.2 (depending on the material)
doors

Building Regulations

The Building Regulations for England, Wales and Scotland require that 'reasonable provision shall be made for the conservation of fuel and power in dwellings by limiting the heat loss through the fabric of the building'. In practice, this means not exceeding the maximum U-values (see previous page) unless you can show that your proposed solution satisfies the general requirement.

Over the years, Building Regulations (and before them, local bylaws) have steadily raised the levels of insulation required in new houses: lofts, for example, needed only 25mm (1in) of insulation before the 1976 Regulations came into force. After that this went up to 50mm (2in) and subsequently to 100mm (4in) and later 200mm (8in). Now you need 250mm (10in). So, many older houses are seriously under-insulated by modern standards.

In the past, you needed to worry about Building Regulations only when you were building an extension to your home (or converting the loft or other space for living in). But since April 2002, Part L of the Building Regulations – which deals with conservation of fuel and power – requires householders to install more energy-efficient options if they are replacing windows, heating boilers or hot-water cylinders.

The Building Control Department at your local authority will be able to provide information on complying with the Building Regulations. In certain instances you are required to employ a 'competent person' – if you are fitting a gas boiler you must use a member of CORGI (the Council for Registered Gas Installers), who may be required to provide a certificate of compliance.

The Energy Saving Trust's* Energy Efficiency Installer Network is an audited UK network of qualified heating, glazing and insulation installers.

Draught-proofing

Draught-proofing doors and windows is simple. In a typical house, it will cost £35 to £80 if you do the work yourself, giving a saving in fuel costs of around £15 to £25 a year. This measure should pay for itself within three or four years.

A wide selection of different types of draught excluder is available. Most of them are clearly labelled with the size of gap they are designed to fill. They normally come with instructions, but if you are uncertain about how to fit them, any good DIY book will have a section on draught-proofing.

When thinking about draught-proofing your home, remember to consider ventilation. This is particularly important in rooms that contain heating appliances or those which are prone to condensation (such as kitchens and bathrooms). See the boxes about ventilation and condensation on the following pages for more details. If you are unsure about where you should fit draught-proofing, check first with the Energy Saving Trust (EST)★ or your local Energy Efficiency Advice Centre (listed at the back of this book).

Draught-proofing doors and windows
Preparation
Measure the perimeter of the doors and windows to work out the quantity of materials needed, and measure the thickness of the maximum gap to be filled.

The cheapest option for draught-proofing around wooden casement doors and windows is to use a self-adhesive foam strip, which sticks to the rebate and compresses to eliminate draughts when closed. Metal or plastic strips with a brush or wiper seal down one side are also available: although more expensive, they last a lot longer.

The type of seal you need for your windows will depend on the type of window you have and the size of gap you are trying to fill. Sliding sash windows are the most complex to draught-proof: the best solution is usually a brush-type excluder fitted to the frame. The bottom of an outside door will need draught-proofing with a brush-type or hinged-flap-type seal along the bottom. You can also get seals to stop the wind whistling through your letterbox. Internal doors need less robust draught excluders: you can get types which fit to the door or the threshold. If you leave a gap at the top of internal doors, this allows air to pass from room to room without draughts.

Look out for products that conform to British Standard BS7386.

Procedure
1 Clean and dry all the window and door rebates before applying any adhesive product.
2 Cut the draught-proofing strip to length, place it on the frame and push it against the opening part of the door or window. Then

nail or pin the strip to the frame. Always apply nails or pins within 25mm (1in) of the end of a draught strip.

3 For outside doors, cut the brush or hinged-flap seal to equal the door width (minus about 5mm). Position the carrier and check that it doesn't hit the door-frame as you open the door. If it does hit the frame, cut it shorter. You will then need to close

Ventilation

Ensuring adequate ventilation is extremely important when draught-proofing your home. You can no longer rely on gaps around doors and windows to provide a flow of air and must therefore achieve controlled ventilation by some of the following means:

- permanent ventilation openings for fuel-burning appliances
- background ventilation through trickle ventilators and air-bricks
- rapid ventilation by opening windows
- extractor fans.

If you use bottled-gas or paraffin heaters, do not draught-proof any windows in the house. You can draught-proof windows in kitchens and bathrooms, but at least one window must be able to be opened unless an extractor fan is fitted.

Permanent ventilation openings

Unless heating appliances are fitted with a balanced flue, which draws fresh air from the outside and expels exhaust gases through the same fitting, they need air from inside a room to operate safely and the room should therefore have permanent ventilation.

Most modern boilers (and many gas fires and heaters) have a balanced flue. The size of permanent ventilation openings is set out in the Building Regulations. You could consult a qualified heating contractor for advice (by law, you must use a qualified gas installer for gas appliances). In older houses the original ventilators may have been papered over.

Background ventilation

To achieve a constant supply of fresh air without draughts, you can fit both ends of the carrier to stop the brush slipping out. Put the brush in place so the seal rests on the floor covering and fix it in place.

4 Fit a letterbox cover to the inside of the front door, making sure that letters can still pass through easily. You could fit a keyhole cover too.

'trickle' ventilators into the tops of windows or their frames, or have air-bricks in outside walls fitted with 'hit-and-miss' ventilator grilles.

Rapid ventilation

All rooms should ideally have opening windows with an opening area not less than one-twentieth of the room's floor area. If a room containing a WC does not have an opening window, it should have an extractor fan wired to come on with the light switch.

Extract ventilation

In kitchens, bathrooms and utility rooms, you ideally need some kind of extractor fan (or cooker hood in a kitchen). This should have an extract facility of 30 litres per second for kitchens and utility rooms; 15 litres per second for bathrooms. Tumble-driers should be individually vented to the outside.

Further ventilation

Specific ventilation measures can be taken to avoid condensation in certain areas of the house (see box overleaf). Where a fireplace has been bricked up, for example, a ventilator needs to be fitted both at room level and in the chimney, to prevent condensation inside the flue (which will cause staining). In lofts, all gaps around pipes and wires leading down to the house should be sealed, the loft hatch should be draught-proofed, and additional ventilation, such as eaves ventilators, roof-tile ventilators and air-bricks in gable-end walls, should be fitted if necessary. Warning: it is important not to block the air-bricks that are installed at ground level to ventilate the space under suspended timber floors.

Condensation

One of the more serious problems that can be caused by inadequate ventilation is condensation. This occurs when warm, moist air hits a cold surface, such as an outside wall or a window – the water vapour in the air forms tiny water droplets on the surface (familiar as the misting on single-glazed windows). This can lead to black mould on walls (which can contribute to respiratory diseases such as bronchitis and asthma) and rotting timbers in the roof or floor spaces, which may go unnoticed until it is too late.

The most important steps you can take to prevent condensation are reducing the amount of moisture produced in the home, and improving ventilation and insulation (follow the advice in this chapter). You can cut down on moisture in the following ways.

- **Drying clothes** 6lbs of spun washing produces 10 pints of moisture when drying. If you use a tumble-drier make sure it is vented to the outside. If you have to dry clothes indoors, open the window and shut the door.
- **In the bathroom** Having a bath produces two pints of moisture. If you have an extractor fan in the bathroom, remember to use it. Alternatively open a window for half an hour after bathing or showering.
- **In the kitchen** Cooking by gas for three hours produces three pints of moisture – in addition to vapour produced by boiling water for vegetables and the like. Use an extractor fan or extracting cooker hood, if you have one, or open the window to let the moisture out. If you have trickle vents above the windows, keep them open all the time.

Hot-water pipe and cylinder insulation

Lagging your hot-water pipes and cylinder will mean that the water inside loses heat less quickly. An airing cupboard will still be warm enough to air clothes after the cylinder and pipes have been lagged.

Ideally, a hot-water cylinder should be of the pre-insulated type with factory-installed foam insulation. If it is bare copper, or has only a poorly fitting jacket, it will lose a lot of heat. Fortunately, a new insulating jacket and pipe insulation are cheap, easy to fit and pay for themselves very quickly.

Lagging the hot-water cylinder

A hot-water cylinder jacket should cost no more than £10 and will save between £10 and £20 a year in fuel costs.

Preparation

Measure the height and diameter (the circumference divided by 3.14) of your hot-water cylinder and buy a jacket the correct size. Look for products that conform to British Standard BS5615.

Procedure

1 Turn off the hot-water heating system and allow the cylinder and pipes to cool before you carry out the work. You may be able to leave an old jacket in place and fit the new one over it.
2 Tie the tops of the jacket segments tightly around the pipe at the top of the cylinder and place them evenly around the cylinder so it is totally covered. Pipes from the cylinder, the cylinder thermostat and any immersion-heater heads should be between segments. Elsewhere the segments should overlap slightly. Do not cover any electric wires leading to thermostats or immersion heaters.
3 Fix the jacket in place with the straps provided, making sure that the fixing straps do not compress the insulation too much, as this will reduce its insulating qualities. Check that there is a gap of no more than 20mm (¾in) from the bottom of the jacket to the bottom of the cylinder.

Lagging hot-water pipes

If you lag the pipes that deliver your hot water for the whole of their length, you will find that you can turn your hot water temperature down a little. There will also be less time to wait at the tap before hot water arrives. Insulating hot-water pipes should cost less than £10 and save £5 to £10 a year.

Preparation

There are two key areas you need to insulate:

- between the boiler and the hot-water cylinder
- all hot-water pipes, especially the first metre of hot-water pipe from the hot-water cylinder to the taps.

Measure the length of pipes to be lagged. There are various kinds of insulation available. The most convenient is pre-formed split foam tubes: 20–25mm (1in) is the minimum thickness you should use. If it is not practicable to use pre-formed foam of this thickness because the pipes are awkwardly sited or too close together, loft insulation material can be wrapped around the pipes instead. You will need suitable tape to seal the foam tubing and to join lengths; electrical insulating tape is ideal. Cut the insulating tubes at tee-joints and corners to fit, making neat mitre joints.

Procedure

1　Turn off the water-heating system and allow the pipes to cool before you carry out any work on them.
2　Remove any old or damaged pipe insulation.
3　If using foam tubes, make sure the insulation is properly split all along its length and slide it on to the pipes. Try to avoid leaving any gaps where pipes are held in pipe clips or pass through walls. Be particularly careful to shape the insulation at junctions and bends. Seal the split with electrical insulating tape.

Loft insulation

Loft insulation could save you up to 20 per cent on your heating bills. Installing loft insulation yourself is likely to cost around £100 to £150 (or £300 to £400 if you employ a contractor), but should save you £50 to £75 a year. It will take about two to three years to start saving on your outlay, or four to six years if you employ someone else.

If your loft is already insulated, it may just need topping up to the recommended thickness (see below), although old, damaged or thin insulation is not worth keeping. If you are not competent with DIY, a builder will be able to install it for you. Members of the National Insulation Association (NIA)★ are specialist contractors. The NIA can provide a list of installers as well as literature on cavity wall, external wall and loft insulation, and draught-proofing. You may also be eligible for a grant or free loft insulation – see Appendix II.

To meet modern building standards, loft insulation should be 250mm (10in) thick. If yours is less than 150mm (6in) it will be worthwhile topping it up. Heat will also be lost through the joists, so remember to lay most of the top layer of insulation across them.

This will mean that the loft can no longer be used for storage – unless you build up the loft joists. You will, in any case, have to build up some loft joists in order to provide a boarded area for access to water tanks.

Insulating material for lofts comes in two main forms, matting or loose-fill. Mineral wool matting, or 'quilt', is the most common and is usually sold in rolls 400mm (16in) wide. Loose-fill insulation (mineral wool or cellulose) can be blown into the loft by professional installers, or poured between the joists (a DIY job). See Chapter 8 for information about 'green' insulation materials.

Look out for products conforming to British Standard BS5803.

Preparation

Ensure that you have adequate lighting so that you can work safely in the loft. Always use crawling boards and never step on the ceiling between the joists. Identify potential hazards (such as electrical cables and loose boards) before you start. Check that the loft is ventilated from spaces at the eaves or from ventilators in the roof itself. If not, this has to be rectified before the loft is insulated or the timbers in your loft may suffer condensation damage.

Squeezing rolls of insulation through a small loft hatch can release mineral wool fibres or glass fibre strands which can irritate exposed skin, so it is important to wear proper gloves, protective clothing, a dust-proof face mask and goggles. These are all available from good DIY stores.

Never tear the matting as this releases fibres. It is best to use a knife to cut it, but be careful not to cut electrical wires by accident. For extra safety, do not use a knife with a metal handle.

Give yourself plenty of room to work safely. If possible, empty your loft space completely – or at least enough so you can work in sections.

Measure:

- the space between the joists (to determine the width of quilt needed), unless you are topping up existing insulation
- the depth of the joists. If these are less than 250mm (10in) deep, you will have to build up the joists to create a boarded area to retain access to the loft space, as the minimum thickness recommended for insulation in the Building Regulations is

250mm. In any case you'll need to maintain access to all the tanks in the loft

- the length and width of your loft – multiply these together to get the approximate area you need to cover
- the size of your loft hatch, to ensure that you will be able to get the packs of insulation through it.

Procedure

1 Lay the insulation, starting in the eaves at the corner furthest from the loft hatch. Do not tuck the quilt right into the eaves but stop short so that there is at least a 50mm (2in) air gap. Gently press the quilt down to prevent air movement below the quilt.

2 Where strengthening timbers cross the joists, cut the quilt with a knife and butt the two ends together under the obstruction. Wherever possible, position electrical cables above the insulation – but be careful not to force cables out of the way.

3 Do not insulate under cold-water tanks – lead the quilt up the side of the tank and lap the tank jacket (see step 6 below) over the quilt ends. This allows warmth from the house to reach the tank and prevent it from freezing. Where extractor fans or recessed lights are fixed through the ceiling and protrude into the loft space, trim the quilt around the fitting, leaving a gap of 150mm (6in) all round.

4 Insulate the loft hatch cover with rigid polystyrene held in place with adhesive or a piece of quilt enclosed in polythene, secured at the edges with staples. Draught-proof the loft hatch using a simple foam excluder.

5 Once the loft is insulated it will be colder than before (as it will receive less heat from your home) so you must insulate all pipes and tanks in the loft to prevent them from freezing. If insulating pipes with pre-formed foam is difficult because they are too close together, another method is to wrap a section of loft insulation quilt around the pipe(s). Note that cold-water pipes in other exposed areas (under floors or in outbuildings) should also be insulated for protection against frost.

6 For the cold-water tank, ready-made jackets of mineral-fibre quilt enclosed in polythene are available. You can also use rigid poly-styrene slabs or loft quilt wrapped in polythene. If the tank has no lid, buy one and insulate it along with the rest of the tank. Use broad tapes to tie the insulation in place – thin cord may cut

through it. If you are using a ready-made water tank jacket, fit it so that the open side is at the inlet pipe to the float-operated valve. Lay the jacket over the tank so that the sides are fully covered and secure in place with tapes. Make sure that there are no loose fibres.

Wall insulation

Insulating the exterior walls of your home can save you up to 20 per cent on your heating costs. It will also cut down noise, reduce condensation on wall surfaces and give a more even temperature within the home. There are different types of insulation for solid and cavity walls; most need a specialist contractor to install them.

Insulating different types of house

Older houses in the UK have solid masonry walls 230mm (9in) or 340mm (13½in) thick. Some bricks will be laid sideways rather than lengthways. Such buildings can either be insulated on the outside (external wall insulation) or on the inside (internal wall insulation). External wall insulation is more appropriate for solid walls with a rendered finish.

Most houses built since about 1930 have cavity walls: two 'leaves' of masonry with a gap in between to prevent water getting in. Modern houses built with cavity walls have the gap filled with solid insulation 'batts' made of glass fibre or polystyrene; in older houses, the gaps can be filled from the outside (cavity wall insulation). Cavity walls are around 280mm (11in) thick, and all the bricks on the outside are laid lengthways.

Modern timber-frame houses have 280mm(11in)-thick walls. The outer wall is usually brick (with all the bricks laid lengthways), with an inner wall built from a timber frame already containing a thick insulating layer. Under no circumstances should these be additionally insulated with cavity foam insulation. Timber-frame walls sound hollow when you tap them on the inner (room) side. If you are in any doubt as to what type of walls you have, check with a builder or architect.

Cavity wall insulation

More heat is lost through the walls than through any other part of the house. Yet only one in five homes with cavity walls have cavity wall insulation.

Cavity wall insulation is likely to cost around £450 or more, but you should save £75 to £150 a year on your heating bills. It should take about three years before you start to recoup your initial expenditure – you will also feel the benefits in terms of more even temperatures within rooms.

Insulating cavity walls is a fairly straightforward procedure with very little in the way of internal or external disruption to the building, but you will need a qualified specialist contractor to install the insulation for you, who should be able to do the job in a day. The Energy Saving Trust (EST)★ or your local Energy Efficiency Advice Centre (listed at the back of this book) will be able to provide you with details of qualified contractors in your area. Choose those who are members of the National Insulation Association (NIA)★.

Various grants are available that cover cavity wall insulation. Appendix II, at the end of this book, details a number of these.

External wall insulation

Houses with solid walls have no cavity to fill. The usual option here is to add insulating material to the outside surface of the walls, weatherproofing it with a decorative finish. However, this is a professional job and can therefore be expensive. Exterior insulation is most appropriate if your house is rendered, especially if the general quality of the outside building is not of a high standard and needs repair anyway. External wall insulation is more expensive than cavity wall insulation, but should be equally effective.

Internal wall insulation

For listed buildings or those in conservation areas, external wall insulation will not be an option. If brickwork or stonework is particularly attractive, insulation material can be added to the interior surface of the exterior walls. North-facing walls of rooms you use most often might also need to be insulated.

This is a job which an experienced DIY householder might attempt. The cost will depend on the method chosen (and whether you employ a contractor), but you should save £75 to £150 a year on heating, and will start to recover costs about six years after your initial spend.

Internal wall insulation can be done in two ways:

- by covering the inside wall surface with insulating plasterboard
- by building a new timber-frame wall against the inside face of the masonry, placing fibreglass batts between the timbers and covering the whole frame with plasterboard.

With either method, door and window openings will need to be re-lined (and mouldings such as architraves re-positioned) and all electrical fittings (light switches, sockets and wall lights) on the outside wall will have to be removed and re-fitted.

If you choose internal insulation, it is probably cheaper (if you are using a contractor) to do it all at once. If you do it room by room, however, this allows you the flexibility of redecorating as you go.

Window insulation

The cheapest and easiest way of insulating your windows is to use thick curtains and keep them closed at night. Windows are often insulated by double glazing – having two panes of glass instead of one. However, only around 10 per cent of heat is lost through windows and you are unlikely to save much more than half of this unless you go for triple glazing or sealed units using low-emissivity glass. Most types of double glazing are expensive and rarely cost-effective in terms of energy-saving, although you may think that the other benefits (reduced noise, for example) are worth paying for – see overleaf.

Professionally installed double glazing can cost thousands of pounds but is an option worth considering as a home improvement measure when your windows need replacing. Simple DIY double glazing gives many of the same benefits and should pay for itself in five years or less.

Using curtains

At night, you can save a lot of heat loss through windows by having thick or lined curtain material. You can reduce the down-draughts from between the window and the curtains by using a 'box' pelmet which gives a snug fit around the top of the curtain. If a radiator is fitted below a window, either tuck the curtain behind the radiator, or fit a shelf above it (see page 74) so that the warm convection current from the radiator does not go up behind the curtain and escape.

Double glazing

Double glazing works by trapping a layer of air, or other insulating gas, between two panes of glass. The minimum distance between the two panes is important: the ideal gap is about 12mm (½in). If the main reason for installing double glazing is to reduce noise (from a road or aircraft), a larger gap of 100–200mm (4–8in) will be more effective and reduce the heat insulation effect by only a minimal amount.

Besides saving energy, double glazing reduces, and in some cases eliminates, the amount of condensation on windows. Noise from outside is lessened and there will be a significant decrease in down-draughts, allowing radiators to be positioned elsewhere in the room other than under the window. It also improves comfort by balancing out the temperature across the room and eliminating the 'cold zone' next to the window, and it can improve security.

Double glazing can be one of two types – sealed units or secondary glazing.

Sealed units

In a sealed unit, two panes of glass are permanently sealed together with an air gap (sometimes gas-filled) between them. It is sometimes possible to fit a sealed unit in place of an existing single pane of glass, but most sealed units are used in replacement windows (see below) in new timber, plastic, aluminium or steel frames, which are fitted in place of the existing frames. The most effective sealed units are those which use low-emissivity (Low E) glass for one of the panes. This has a reflective coating which reflects heat back into the room.

Replacement windows

Replacement windows are complete units which replace your existing windows, frame and all, and incorporate sealed units. The new frames can be made of timber (hardwood or softwood), painted aluminium, painted steel or plastic.

- Timber has the advantage of being a good insulator, but needs regular maintenance (particularly softwood) to keep it looking good.
- Aluminium has the advantage of having thin sections and of being

---

Secondary glazing

With secondary glazing, a second pane of glass (or plastic), which is either fixed or can be opened, is installed on the inside of the existing window. You can have secondary double glazing professionally installed on a separate frame within the existing reveal (a good solution if noise is your main concern); some DIY systems can be installed like this. Most DIY double glazing systems, however, are attached to the existing window or frame.

DIY double glazing

There are many kits available for you to add your own secondary glazing. The simplest is a roll of clear plastic film, which you stick to the window with double-sided adhesive tape and make taut with a hairdryer. This will cut down heat loss effectively, but needs to be replaced every year. More durable are sheets of clear plastic, which you secure to the window (or a separate frame) with magnetic strips or clips and which can be easily removed for cleaning or summer storage. There are also sliding systems, which have their own frame.

Floor insulation

Floors, especially bare floorboards, can account for 15 per cent of heat loss in a home. The easiest way to reduce this loss is to cover the floor with underlay, carpet, a thick timber floor covering or cork tiles. You may also be able to insulate a suspended timber floor from below by pushing insulating material cut to joist width (such as expanded polystyrene sheets or semi-rigid mineral wool mats) between the joists.

---

low-maintenance, but needs a 'thermal break' built in to prevent condensation on the frame.

- Steel also needs a thermal break and may be limited in the thickness of sealed unit it can take.
- Plastic has the advantage of being low-maintenance, with similar profiles and appearance to the timber it may be replacing.

Replacement windows now have to comply with Building Regulations, which will almost certainly mean having low emissivity (Low E) glass for one of the panes of the sealed units.

To insulate from the top, lift the entire flooring (floorboards or chipboard sheets) and lay netting across the joist. This can then support rolls of loft insulation material which you fit between the joists before the floorboards or sheets are put back. For savings in fuel bills to cover the cost of floor insulation (starting at £100) may take six to eight years. For most people, the answer to draughty timber floors is to fill the gaps between floorboards with wood filler, papier-mâché or thin slivers of wood. Gaps under skirting boards can be filled with sealant (mastic) or covered with wooden beading.

Do not block air-bricks in external walls – they provide vital ventilation to the under-floor space, preventing woodworm and rot.

If the floor is solid concrete, adding insulation will involve re-laying or raising the whole floor. This is likely to be very expensive.

Space heating

Heating and hot water account for over half the cost of the average household fuel bill. Space heating is the biggest single user of energy in the home, making it one of the most profitable to tackle. Water heating is a smaller user (perhaps one-fifth of the amount used by space heating), though changes here will still be worthwhile. Some cost reductions will result from changes to the main heating system (particularly if you change the boiler).

There are two main types of space heating system. The more common is a 'wet' system – that is, one where water is heated by a boiler and circulated around the house to heat the rooms via radiators. The boiler is commonly powered by gas but may be powered by other fuels, such as oil or liquefied petroleum gas (LPG). This type can accurately be described as 'central heating', as the heat comes from a central source. The other type is individual, or unit, heaters. The most common type of unit heaters are electric storage heaters that take in heat at night (using a low-rate tariff) and give it out during the day. These are found in 'all-electric' homes. Another type, gas wall heaters with balanced flues, is more cost-effective than electric storage radiators, but rare.

Although using gas to heat rooms and water results in less carbon dioxide emissions than using electricity, it is still possible to make further reductions by making more efficient use of heating.

Generally, systems that use a boiler or linked gas wall heaters have the potential to be more energy-efficient as you have more precise temperature and timing control. Using electric storage heaters will always involve a degree of guesswork; they may give out more or less heat than is needed and not always at the right times.

An alternative to conventional systems – or an auxiliary to them – is a solid-fuel stove. This time-honoured method of heating is simple and attractive to many people and, with modern stove designs, is clean and efficient. Solid-fuel systems that include hot-water heating and central heating components are available, and you can get 'clean burn' stoves for use in smokeless zones. For more information contact the Solid Fuel Association★.

Central heating systems

When assessing the energy-efficiency of a wet central heating system there are two elements that need to be considered: the components (mainly the boiler and the radiators) and the controls. As far as components are concerned, the greatest potential for energy saving in a central heating system is in replacing the boiler.

Is your system the right size?

If central heating is already installed in your home, but you have improved insulation and draught-proofing, it is likely that your heating system will be over-sized. This does not mean you will have to rip it all out and start from scratch, simply that the boiler size can be reduced when you next have to replace it.

If you want to replace your radiators because, say, you want more modern-looking ones, you may be able to have fewer and smaller radiators, and avoid having them under the windows if you have installed double glazing. If you have insulated thoroughly, it may even be possible to do away with radiators in some upstairs rooms, and to rely on heat finding its way up from the ground floor.

Choosing the right system

If you are putting in a central heating system for the first time, gas offers the widest choice of high-efficiency boilers and oil is the best option if gas is not available.

Making the right choice can make a big difference in terms of carbon dioxide emissions as well as money saved. The best boilers for low carbon dioxide emissions are natural gas boilers, with the most efficient of all being the condensing boiler. Condensing boilers (see box below) maintain a high efficiency even at low loads, with their 'cycling' efficiency being close to 90 per cent compared with 70–75 per cent for new conventional gas boilers.

Many central heating systems are most efficient when they are working at maximum load. This means that if the system is designed for the coldest day it will be working less efficiently on all other days. However, the latest designs of boilers and their controls are now beginning to address this problem.

For an up-to-the-minute guide to seasonal efficiencies of domestic boilers in the UK, get a copy of the Energy Saving Trust's *The Little Blue Book of Boilers*, which lists all the latest high-performance models. Alternatively, if you have access to the Internet, you can visit www.boilers.org.uk.

For a copy of the comprehensive *The Domestic Heating and Hot Water Guide to the Building Regulations 2001 – Part L1* contact the Energy Saving Trust (EST)★. Alternatively, visit www.centralheating.co.uk. You can also contact the Building Research Establishment's (BRE)★ Housing Energy Efficiency Best Practice programme for advice; the *Good Practice Guide 301 (Domestic heating and hot water: a choice of fuel and system type)* and *General Information Leaflet 59: Central Heating System Specifications (CheSS)*, are available from them.

Replacing your boiler

Modern boilers are not only more energy-efficient but are also more compact, helping to save on space as well. Replacing a 15-year-old boiler could save you up to 20 per cent on your fuel bills, or 32 per cent if you install a condensing boiler. Condensing boilers are the most efficient boilers because they recover more heat from flue gases that is normally wasted. It is worth considering one if you have to replace your boiler.

Although condensing boilers are more expensive, the extra cost compared with installing a conventional boiler should be recovered in three or four years – after that you'll make greater savings each year.

Another option you have when replacing an old boiler is to install

Efficiency

To keep a boiler working to its maximum efficiency, it is important to have it serviced regularly. You will save at least some of the servicing costs in reduced fuel bills.

You also need to protect your systems against internal corrosion, which is caused by having steel radiators in conjunction with copper pipes. As well as rusting (and eventual 'pinholing') of radiators, corrosion causes sludge build-up in the system, which reduces efficiency and may cause noise. It can be prevented by adding a corrosion-proofer to the system; existing systems need to be cleansed first to get rid of the sludge.

Radiators

Radiators are an important part of the central heating system. They can be adjusted to give optimum output and made more efficient by means of a few simple measures.

Reflective radiator foil

Putting foil behind radiators that are against an outside wall will reflect heat back into the room. This is particularly effective for solid-walled houses. You can use normal kitchen foil, or buy specially designed foil panels with a foam backing from a DIY store,

a combination (combi) boiler, which provides instant hot water as well as space heating (see 'Water heating' on page 79). These are more expensive than conventional boilers (because they have a greater capacity) and may cost more to install if a lot of other plumbing work is involved, but you may think the advantage of having hot water always available justifies the extra cost. Some condensing combination boilers are available that will repay their extra cost in a very few years.

If you are replacing your boiler, it may be possible to change fuels – from LPG to oil, for example – but remember that both oil and LPG need a storage tank and that solid fuel needs constant attention. To change from electricity would mean replacing the whole system.

fixing it to the wall with double-sided sticky pads or heavy-duty, fungicidal wallpaper paste. Each square metre of foil should save £2 a year in fuel costs so this measure should pay for itself in one to two years, depending on how much you spend.

Remember to turn off the heating system and allow the radiators to cool before you carry out any work on them.

Putting shelves above radiators

Putting shelves above your radiators may sound odd, but it ensures that as much heat as possible is deflected out into your rooms. The shelf should be slightly above the radiator. It will also help if you avoid putting furniture directly in front of radiators.

Fitting radiator shelves saves only around £10 to £15 a year, so it could take some time to pay back the cost of the shelves.

You can buy ready-made radiator shelves, which simply rest on the radiator, or you can fit brackets for your own shelf material. You should also be careful to use a material that will not warp or discolour with the heat from the radiator. Be sure to check for hidden pipes and electrical cables before you start drilling into any walls.

Before fixing the shelf to the brackets, apply foam draught excluder along the back of the shelf so that there is no gap between it and the wall. This will prevent hot air from getting past and discolouring the wall above.

Bleeding radiators

If air gets into a central heating system, it can collect at the top of the radiators and reduce efficiency. Radiators need to be bled – to remove the air– at least at the beginning of each heating season and more often if the water has had to be changed.

It is easy to tell if a radiator needs bleeding. When the heating is on, feel the top and the bottom of the radiator. If the top is cooler than the bottom then there is air in the radiator preventing the hot water from rising to the top. Note that if the bottom is colder than the top, it indicates sludge build-up due to corrosion.

Turn off your heating system so that the pump is not running and the water is cool. To bleed your radiator you will need a radiator key. You can get one for a few pence at a DIY or hardware store. Take care to protect your carpets as the water being released from the radiator may be dirty.

Get a cloth and place it under the bleed valve, which you will find at one end of the radiator, at the top. Insert the key and gently turn it anticlockwise. Open the valve just enough to let the air out, but be very careful not to completely unscrew it. You will hear a hissing sound as the air releases. When the air is all gone the hissing stops and water will run out. At this point re-tighten the valve by turning the key clockwise.

Balancing radiators

A radiator performs best when the difference in temperature of the water coming in and going out (flow and return) is 11°C (typically this is 82°C flow and 71°C return). To achieve these temperatures, the radiator has to be balanced – that is, the water flow through it must be adjusted by using a spanner to open or close the lockshield valve at one end (the one normally covered up) with the normal handwheel valve fully open. For more details see *The Which? Book of Plumbing and Central Heating*.

Central heating controls

You can save up to 20 per cent on your annual fuel costs by improving your central heating controls. Timeswitches, programmers, thermostats and thermostatic radiator valves are all control features that allow you to have the room temperatures you want, when you want them, and turn the system on and off automatically. If your system doesn't have these controls, they can be fitted; if it does, they can often be upgraded. You will recoup costs after between two and eight years, depending on your existing controls and what you fit.

Most heating control improvements require both electrical and plumbing work and therefore should be attempted only by experienced DIY experts. For further information about improvements to heating controls and for a list of local energy efficiency professionals, contact your local Energy Efficiency Advice Centre (listed at the back of this book).

Electricians will be on the roll of the National Inspection Council for Electrical Installation Contractors (NICEIC)★ or be members of the Electrical Contractors' Association (ECA)★. Plumbers will be members of the Institute of Plumbing (IoP)★,

Heating and Ventilating Contractors' Association (HVCA)★ or the Association of Plumbing and Heating Contractors (APHC)★.

Using your central heating system efficiently means that you can get the best performance from the system for the least cost. To do this you need to know how to work the heating controls properly.

Timeswitches and programmers

Timeswitches and programmers are a means of switching the boiler and pump on and off at preset times. This can be one of the most important ways in which you can save energy – you save money by having heat only when you need it. Coupled with good all-round insulation, the length of time the boiler needs to be working will be considerably reduced.

A simple on/off timeswitch may be all you need if you have a combination boiler (see page 73), but a system which heats both ra-diators and a hot-water cylinder needs a programmer with separate controls for the hot water and central heating. Old-fashioned electro-mechanical programmers can be replaced with modern electronic programmers, which allow totally separate control for hot water and heating, and different programmes for weekdays and weekends. Programmers cost from £30 to £50 (£80 to £100 if installed). You can probably save around five per cent of your heating costs by adding a programmer, which should pay for itself in three to four years.

Room thermostats

A room thermostat controls the running of the heating system based on the temperature of the room it is in. It is usually placed in your most frequently used room or in the hallway and brings the boiler and pump on when the air temperature at the thermostat falls below the set temperature, turning them off when it rises. If no room thermostat is fitted and the system relies only on the boiler thermostat, one can easily be added.

Conventional thermostats are inexpensive (they cost £10 to £15, or £60 if installed) and should save around five per cent of heating costs, paying for themselves in two to three years. An existing thermostat can be replaced by a programmable thermostat if you have no programmer or if you have a combination boiler.

The correct setting for the thermostat is 21°C for pensioners and families with young children; between 18–21°C for everyone else. Note that turning up the room thermostat will not heat the room up faster; it will make the whole house hotter and will cost you more in fuel bills.

Thermostatic radiator valves
Thermostatic radiator valves (TRVs) are combined thermostat and valve units which reduce or increase the water flow through the radiators to which they are fitted, according to the temperature in the room. They allow you to have different temperatures in each room, and have three main uses:

- to reduce temperatures in rooms not in use (bedrooms during the day, for example)
- to prevent rooms with additional heating (such as an open fire) from getting too hot
- to compensate for rooms where sunlight during the day increases the heat level.

A thermostatic radiator valve is fitted in place of the handwheel valve. Normally this means draining the whole system, but some TRVs use the existing valve body without the need to do this. Unless you have a boiler energy manager in place of a programmer, you should not fit TRVs to all radiators. Thermostatic radiator valves do not save huge amounts of money – perhaps two to three per cent of your heating bill – but they are inexpensive if you fit them yourself (they cost around £10 each) and should pay for themselves in a few years.

To find the correct setting for the TRV, start with a middle setting and turn down a notch if the room gets too warm and up a notch if it is too cool. If the radiators go cool, and you are warm, this is normal and means the thermostat is doing its job.

Boiler thermostat
Found on the boiler itself, this controls the temperature of the hot water flowing around the pipes to the radiators. The correct setting is High in winter, Low in summer when being used for hot water only.

Cylinder thermostat

Found on the hot-water cylinder, this controls the temperature of the hot water coming out of the taps. The correct setting is 60°C.

Electric storage heaters

If you live in an 'all-electric' home (with no connection to mains gas), it is almost certain that your space heating will be by means of electric storage heaters. These use electricity on a low tariff at night to generate heat, which is then given out slowly during the day. The main problem with this is that you have to anticipate the heating requirement for the following day. If it is milder than expected, you may have too much heat available and if it is colder, you will not have enough and will have to 'top up' with heaters operating on full-price electricity, which is very expensive. A 'combination' heater can be switched to provide (convected) heat on full-price electricity when the stored heat has run out.

Old-fashioned electric storage radiators are very large and fitted with few controls. These can be replaced with modern, slimline electric storage radiators, which have better controls and take up much less space. To replace an electric system with a central heating system means not only installing a boiler, pipework and conventional radiators, but also laying on a gas supply or having an oil tank installed.

Electric storage heater controls

Electric storage heaters are fitted with two controls – one to control the amount of heat taken in at night (the input or charge control) and the other to control the rate at which it is given out during the day (the output control). The input control can be either automatic (auto-set) or manual; the output control (which may be marked 'room temperature' or 'boost') is always controlled by hand.

Combination heaters have the same controls as storage heaters, plus an additional wall switch for when they are used as full-price convector heaters.

Hot tip

By simply lowering the setting on your room thermostat by 1°C you can reduce your heating bill by as much as 10 per cent.

Water heating

An average family of four uses 700–1,200 litres of hot water a week, costing around £100 a year. Heating water can account for about one-tenth of a household's total energy use.

There are several ways to reduce the amount of money spent on hot water heating. The first is to use less heated water – by taking showers rather than baths and by using only full loads in the washing machine and dishwasher. (For more information about water-saving measures see Chapter 5.) The second is to reduce the temperature of hot water used. The third is to improve the insulation of any hot-water cylinders (reducing the energy wasted in keeping water hot), and the last is to improve the hot-water heating controls.

There are two basic types of water heating system: instantaneous, which heats water as required, and storage, which keeps hot water available for use in a cylinder.

Instantaneous systems

These can be of several types:

- a combination (combi) boiler that switches its entire output away from the central heating to heating hot water whenever a tap is turned on
- a multi-point water heater (normally gas) that comes on to heat the hot water whenever a tap in the house is turned on
- a point-of-use heater (gas or electric) which heats the water for just one tap – sometimes this may also store a small amount of hot water
- an electric shower, which has a powerful electric element to heat water direct from the mains.

Storage systems

Hot-water storage systems require a hot-water cylinder – usually in an airing cupboard. This typically holds 120 litres – enough hot water for two hot baths. The water in the cylinder can be heated in one of two ways: by an internal coil connected by pipes to the central heating boiler, or by an electric immersion heater (a 3kW element connected to its own electric circuit). Some cylinders have both methods of heating, with the immersion heater being used in the summer when the boiler can be switched off.

Whenever an immersion heater is used, it should be used on a low-cost tariff, so that the water can be heated cheaply at night (or during certain times of the day). It should also be fitted with an immersion heater timer, or Economy 7 controller, so that it comes on automatically during the cheap-rate period.

Most existing storage systems are fed with cold water from the main tank in the loft. Modern, unvented hot-water storage systems have a specially strengthened cylinder, which takes water direct from the mains. This has many advantages, not least that you can do away with the mains cold water tank (and the risk of its freezing).

Choosing the right system

The choice between an instantaneous system and a storage system depends on the size of your home, the number of people living in it, how frequently it is used and how even or uneven the usage is.

The main advantages of a storage system are that you get a better flow of hot water from the tap and, with an immersion heater, you have an alternative way of heating water should the gas supply fail, the heating oil run out or the boiler stop working. Immersion heaters are best suited to houses with a predictable and low demand for hot water, as once the stored hot water has been used you have to wait until a fresh cylinder-ful is heated. If you use an electric immersion heater to do this during the day, you will normally use full-price electricity for doing this. Provided you keep the temperature down, storage systems do not suffer too much from scale in hard water areas.

The main advantages of instantaneous water systems are that no hot-water cylinder is required, hot water is available all the time and you pay only to heat the water – not to keep it hot. It is also possible to do away with the main cold water tank if all the cold water is taken directly from the mains, with the added bonus of having drinking water available from all cold taps. On the other hand, these systems can suffer badly from scale in hard water areas, the water will be less hot in winter, when the incoming cold water is colder, and they can have a low flow rate – especially if more than one hot tap is being used at a time.

Water heating controls

You may find the following controls on your hot water heating system:

Immersion heater thermostat

This is found under the removable cover of the immersion heater – turn off the electrical supply to the immersion heater before looking for it. You will need a tiny screwdriver to set the thermostat. Choose a setting of 60°C, which should help prevent scale in hard water areas.

Immersion heater on/off switch

Your immersion heater should be wired to a switched fused connection unit that can be used to turn it on and off by hand when required. A better arrangement is to have an immersion heater timer or Economy 7 controller wired between the fused connection unit and the heater, which will bring the heater on during cheap-rate tariff hours.

It is a myth that it costs no more to leave an immersion heater on all the time. Most immersion heater timers and Economy 7 controllers can provide an hour's 'boost' if hot water runs out during the day. If you have a wall control with two switches marked 'bath' and 'basin', it means you have a dual-element heater – 'basin' brings on the shorter heater to heat the top third of the cylinder, while 'bath' brings on the longer heater to heat the whole cylinder.

Hot-water cylinder thermostat

This is an electric switch strapped to the hot-water cylinder that operates when the water inside reaches the required temperature. Normally – in a fully pumped heating system – the thermostat will turn the boiler and pump off (or at least stop the water flow round the water heating circuit) when the water is hot enough. If fitted to a 'gravity' hot water system, a hot-water cylinder thermostat can be wired to a valve which opens or closes on the hot water circuit. A gravity system is best upgraded to a fully pumped operation, so that the hot water heats up faster and its temperature can be better controlled. This will require the fitting of one or two motorised valves, a cylinder thermostat (if none is fitted already) and some re-arrangement of the heating pipework. It is usually a job for a qualified contractor.

Water temperature control

Combination boilers and multi-point instantaneous water heaters have a control which allows you to alter the temperature of the hot water coming out of the taps.

Lighting

Lighting is an area where savings can be made much more quickly and easily than in almost any other. Using energy-efficient lights, making the most of natural light and direct lighting, and controlling light automatically can all help save energy in the home.

Low-energy lights make sense

Lighting usually makes up about 15 per cent of your electricity bill. By replacing one normal 100W light bulb with a 20W energy-saving one you can save up to £10 a year.

It is reckoned that if every household in the UK did this the annual amount of energy saved would be equivalent to that produced by Sizewell B power station. And if the three most-used light bulbs in every house were replaced by low-energy light bulbs, household emissions of carbon dioxide would be cut by nearly seven per cent.

Natural light

When using natural light in our homes we are generally limited by the size and position of existing windows. To ensure there is as much light as possible coming through your windows, try to reduce obstructions that might overshadow them. Keep shrubbery and foliage cut back and curtains pulled away from the windows during the day. Keep windows clean and try to work or read wherever daylight is most available in the room.

Direct lighting

Maximising lighting efficiency in the home means making the most of any available light source and directing it to where it is most needed. So, firstly you need to decide what you need the light for.

For example, provide reading lamps where you need to see detail and reduce background lighting levels with lower-wattage bulbs.

Automatic lighting

Money can be saved if lights are turned on only when they are needed. The main use of automatic systems in the home is external lights activated by passive infra-red sensors and push-button timeswitches (mainly found in shared rented accommodation). This form of lighting has many commercial applications.

Energy-efficient lighting

Up to 95 per cent of the electricity used in a standard light bulb is wasted in heat. At present, the only real energy-saving alternative is compact fluorescent lamps (CFLs). Quartz-halogen light bulbs are also more energy-efficient than standard bulbs, but much less so than CFLs.

Lamps based on light emitting diodes (LEDs), which will be much more energy-efficient than CFLs and also match the aesthetic convenience of standard and quartz-halogen bulbs, are currently being developed and are expected to be available in the near future.

All light bulb packaging now displays an 'A–G scale' energy-efficiency rating similar to that on fridges and other white goods (see Chapter 4). This offers a useful comparison of the different types. For more information see the Market Transformation Programme's★ website at www.mtprog.com.

Standard tungsten and quartz-halogen lamps

Both standard light bulbs and quartz-halogen (also called tungsten-halogen) bulbs produce white light by heating a tungsten filament to literally a 'white hot' temperature. The limiting factors in a standard light bulb are the life of the filament, which evaporates as it gets hotter, and the amount of heat the glass bulb can stand.

In a quartz-halogen light the tungsten filament is encased in a quartz bulb filled with a halogen gas. The gas and the quartz casing allow the filament to be run at a very high temperature, producing more light than a standard bulb for the same wattage, and allowing a much longer filament life. Nevertheless around 90 per cent of the electricity is still wasted in heat.

Quartz-halogen lamps produce a brighter, whiter light than normal tungsten light bulbs. Their light can be focused and directed better than any other light source, which is particularly useful for task lighting. Their main use is in tiny fittings as decorative 'downlighting' and, because they can be operated at low voltage, in bathrooms. Quartz-halogen lamps set within a standard-sized bulb are also available, and these can be used in place of a standard bulb in a central fitting. When used in 'downlight' fittings, however, they provide considerably less light than an open, centrally placed standard light bulb. In general, one 100W standard bulb would provide as much light as four 35–50W distributed quartz-halogen lights.

Some quartz-halogen bulbs operate at low voltage and need a transformer – either a single one built into the light fitting or a separate one connected to the mains and serving several lights. If dimmers are used with quartz-halogen lamps, the dimmer switches will need to be turned on full occasionally, to prolong the life of the lamp.

Compact fluorescent lamps

Compact fluorescent lamps (CFLs) emit white light from a phosphor coating by bombarding it with charged particles from an ionised gas. They use a fifth of the energy required by standard bulbs and convert at least 35 per cent of the electricity into light. They cost more than traditional bulbs (from £3 to £12; typically around £5), but last eight to ten times longer. By replacing your most heavily used bulbs with CFLs you will start making savings very quickly. You should save around £10 a year for each light bulb replaced – and recoup costs within six months.

These lamps fit into the same sockets as normal bulbs and give a warm-coloured light similar to that of standard tungsten lamps, although they do take a few seconds to reach their maximum light intensity. These are best installed where they will be used most – in areas such as living rooms, kitchens and hallways, or places which need to be lit continually – as turning them on and off too often will shorten their life. One minor drawback is that these sorts of lamps cannot, as yet, be used with dimmers. They should also not be used outside as low temperatures can affect their efficiency.

Comparison of light bulb costs

The table below shows the comparative running costs of standard, CFL and quartz-halogen light bulbs. It is difficult to make an exact calculation because with quartz-halogen bulbs the cost of light fittings (and perhaps transformers and wiring) must be included. The table also takes into account the number of bulbs that would be required to give the same overall level of lighting.

The figures assume the bulbs are used for four and a half hours per day, over 8,000 hours (roughly five years' use).

Comparison of running costs over five years of three light bulb types giving the same overall room lighting

Bulb type, wattage and estimated life in hours	Bulbs used in five years (8,000 hours) and their purchase cost	Electricity used in five years (kWh)	Cost of electricity, charged at 8p per unit (kWh)	Total running cost in five years
CFL 20W 8,000 hours	One £5	160kWh	£12.80	£17.80
Standard (tungsten) 100W 1,000 hours	Eight 8 × 50p = £4	800kWh	£64.00	£68.00
Quartz-halogen (decorative/ set) 3 × 50W 4,000 hours	Six 6 × £5 = £30	1200kWh	£96.00	£126.00

Further reading and useful websites

Building Research Establishment. *General Information Leaflet 59: Central Heating System Specifications (CheSS)*

Building Research Establishment. *Good Practice Guide 301 (Domestic heating and hot water: a choice of fuel and system type)*

Energy Saving Trust. *The DIY Guide to Energy Efficiency.* 2000

Energy Saving Trust. *Is Your Home Behaving Badly?* 2001

Energy Saving Trust. *The Little Blue Book of Boilers* (6th ed). 2002

Harland, E. *Eco-Renovation – The ecological home improvement guide.* Green Books Ltd, 1993

Holloway, D. *The Which? Book of Plumbing & Central Heating.* Which? Books, 2001

National Energy Action. *Energy in the Home.* (3rd ed). 1996

www.boilers.org.uk Boiler efficiency database

www.centralheating.co.uk The Central Heating Information Council

www.mtprog.com Market Transformation Programme (MTP) – a strategic policy unit run by Defra

www.solidfuel.co.uk The Solid Fuel Association

Chapter 4

Household appliances and energy efficiency

As well as using energy to heat and light our homes, we consume considerable amounts running domestic appliances. These include 'white goods', such as washing machines, cookers and fridges, and 'brown goods', such as televisions, telephones and personal computers. Our kitchens, in particular, tend to be full of energy-hungry gadgets.

Fridges and freezers use the most energy as they are plugged in 365 days of the year, 24 hours a day, seven days a week. In a typical household they account for about 17 per cent of the overall electricity bill. Cookers, washing machines, tumble-driers and dishwashers also use a large proportion of our domestic energy, so if you are thinking of replacing any of these appliances it pays to buy the most energy-efficient models. Small differences in the daily energy consumption of some appliances can add up to big differences in running costs over the course of a year. So although your ten-year-old washing machine may be working perfectly well, it may be wasting energy and water.

Of course, we cannot be expected to rush out and replace all our old machines with super-energy-efficient ones. But we can use the machines we already own more efficiently.

To start with, we can think about how much energy we consume when we use appliances. People have different habits with regard to how often they use appliances, but being aware of the running costs of some common appliances can provide an incentive to cut back on their use.

Comparison of power usage of electrical appliances

The table below shows the amount of electricity used by different appliances. One unit of electricity, as shown on your fuel bill, is 1kWh (see Chapter 2 for more about measuring electricity consumption). The price of a unit of electricity will be shown on your fuel bill, and is usually about 7 pence.

The wattage of electrical appliances varies from one model to another. This table is based on typical appliances found in homes, not on the most efficient models new to the market.

Appliance	Amount of electricity used
Cold appliances Freezer (upright or chest) Fridge/freezer Fridge	About 1 to 1.5 units a day About 1.5 units a day Less than 1 unit a day
Heating/hot-water appliances Convector heater (2kW) Electric fire (2kW) Infra-red heater (1kW) Oil-filled radiator (500W) Panel heater (1.5 kW) Fan heater (3kW)	½ hour's warmth – 1 unit ½ hour's warmth – 1 unit 1 hour's warmth – 1 unit 2 hours' warmth – 1 unit 40 minutes' warmth – 1 unit 20 minutes' warmth – 1 unit
Wet appliances Dishwasher Tumble-drier Washing machine	One full load – about 1.5 units Full load of cottons – about 3.5 units Full load of synthetics – about 2 units Load at 40°C – less than 1 unit Load at 60°C – about 1 unit
Cooking appliances Cooker and hob Kettle Microwave (850W) Toaster	About 1.5 units a day 12 pints of boiling water – about 1 unit 20 minutes on full power – less than 0.5 unit 60 slices of toast – about 1 unit
Miscellaneous appliances Single underblanket Extractor fan Hair-drier (500W) Iron Shower (7kW)	1.5 hours a night for 1 week – less than 1 unit 24 hours' use – 1 to 2 units 12 ten-minute sessions – 1 unit 1 hour's use – 0.5 to 1 unit 5-minute shower each day for a week – 4 units

Source: *The Energy Advice Handbook*, Energy Inform, 2003

Energy labelling schemes

A number of schemes exist that indicate the energy efficiency of appliances. These can provide helpful information if you are buying a new product. Some of the schemes are discussed below.

Bear in mind that many retailers can also advise on the energy rating and environmental benefits of new appliances – but watch out for their trying to sell you add-ons and extras you don't need.

EU Energy Label

The emphasis on energy-efficient appliances has, to some extent, been driven by the European Energy Labelling scheme, which is part of a growing commitment by various EU governments to reduce carbon dioxide emissions.

Energy labelling was introduced in the UK in 1995 to cover white goods, and is a useful tool to determine the environmental performance of an appliance. Labels range from 'A' for the most energy efficient to 'G' for the least efficient (see example overleaf).

By law, the EU Energy Label must be displayed on all new domestic washing machines, tumble-driers, combined washer-driers, fridges, freezers and fridge-freezer combinations, and dish-washers which are displayed for sale, hire or hire-purchase. Mail-order catalogues and manufacturers' literature must also contain similar information. From July 2003, air conditioners and electric ovens should also come under the scheme.

The EU Energy Label makes it much easier to make a like-for-like comparison when choosing a new appliance.

How to read the label

The more efficient the product, the less energy it needs to do the job. Hence you save both energy and money. You can use the main 'A–G' scale as a general guide to find the best buy. The following other categories also appear on the label.

The 'energy consumption' indicator represents the 'real' cost to the consumer. This value tells you how much electricity the particular model uses in standard tests. This is given as kWh/year for fridges, kWh/cycle for dishwashers and kWh/kg for washing machines, washer-driers and tumble-driers. You can use this information to work out how much you might save between different machines. Actual savings will depend on how you use the appliance.

Energy

Washing machine

Manufacturer
Model

More efficient

ENERGY SCALE

A
B
C
D
E
F
G

B

Less efficient

Energy consumption kWh'cycle (based on standard test results for 60°C cotton cycle) Actual energy consumption will depend on how the appliance is used	1.05
Washing performance A: higher G: lower	**A** B C D E F G
Spin drying performance A: higher G: lower Spin speed (rpm)	A **B** C D E F G 1400
Capacity (cotton) kg Water consumption	5.0 5.5
Noise (dB(A) re 1 PW) Washing Spinning	5.2 7.0

Further information is continued in product brochures

Specific Product Information

To work out running costs, you need to multiply the number of kWh by the cost per unit of electricity – this will be shown on your electricity bill. In the case of fridges and fridge-freezers, factors such as room temperature will affect energy consumption.

The 'performance' values are represented by an 'A–G' scale which is similar to the main energy efficiency rating. Washing machines are rated for performance in the categories of energy consumption, washing and spin-drying – so a washing machine that has a good spin-drying performance, for example, will save you money and time spent tumble-drying.

The value below performance is 'water consumption'. Some appliances use more water than others. Typically, washing machines use 30 to 65 litres of water per wash, although different wash programmes on the same machine may use different amounts of water. It pays to choose an appliance that uses water as efficiently as possible. For example, a washing machine's wash programme that is designed to use 40 litres per wash rather than 60 litres could significantly reduce a household's water consumption.

The next category is noise. Levels of noise and vibration will vary depending on what surface you put the appliance on. This is particularly the case with washing machines and washer-driers. Manufacturers do not have to provide information on noise but if they do, this will help you choose a quieter model. The lower the number, the quieter the appliance.

Energy Efficiency Recommended logo

The Energy Efficiency Recommended logo is a scheme operated by the Energy Saving Trust (EST)*. The EST uses this label to endorse the most efficient products on the market. Products that are 'A'-rated under the EU Energy Label (see above) may also show this logo.

EU Ecolabel

The European Union Ecolabel (flower symbol) may appear on goods which have a lower environmental impact than similar products performing the same function. Product groups to which the label applies so far include washing machines, dishwashers, fridges, light bulbs, televisions, personal computers and laptops. The scheme is voluntary throughout the 15 member states of the European Union, as well as Norway, Iceland and Liechtenstein. As yet, the EU Ecolabel is not widely seen in the UK on domestic appliances.

Appliances with no labels

By law, the EU Energy Label must be displayed at point of purchase. If an appliance does not have a label, ask the retailer for details. If a mail-order appliance does not have a label, contact your local Trading Standards Department for further information (your local

On-line product information

The Market Transformation Programme (MTP) is a strategic policy unit run by the Department for the Environment, Food and Rural Affairs (Defra)*. It supports eco-labelling, and encourages the appliances industry to supply reliable product information as well as aiming to authority is responsible for enforcing the regulations that cover energy information in mail-order catalogues).

Energy-saving white goods

Refrigeration

When it comes to choosing a fridge or freezer most of us will base our choice on three main considerations: the style of appliance (for example, its size, whether it has both fridge and freezer compartments, etc.); the space available to house it (if your kitchen is small, an upright fridge or fridge-freezer may be your preferred choice); and the sort of features we are prepared to pay for.

One of the most important factors to consider when buying a new cold appliance is its location. If you are planning to put it in an unheated garage or utility room, check whether this would place the appliance outside the manufacturer's recommended temperature range – which could invalidate the manufacturer's warranty (see 'freezers out in the cold', page 95). In addition, condensation can collect on the outside surface, which may deteriorate.

You should also avoid placing cold appliances alongside cookers, tumble-driers or any other direct heat source, such as sunlight. Cold appliances need an adequate amount of ventilation – check the manufacturer's instructions. If you do install a device next to a heat source, make sure you leave a clearance space as recommended by the manufacturer.

All refrigeration products are legally required to carry the EU Energy Label (see page 89), which rates their efficiency. At the time of writing, all new fridges on the market are 'C'-rated or above, and all chest freezers have an 'E' rating or higher.

improve efficiency and standards. The MTP runs the UK Environmental Product Information Consortium, which provides useful advice about the performance of various products and services, including online buyers' guides to refrigeration, heating, ventilation and air-conditioning equipment. Their website at www.ukepic.com contains further details.

Fridges

Most fridges have an interior temperature of between 0°C and 7°C. This is normally controlled by an internal dial. The ideal interior storage temperature is between 3°C and 5°C, as bacterial activity in food is low at these temperatures. Do not be tempted to operate your fridge on a slightly warmer setting to save energy. The amount saved will be small and this poses a potential health risk. It can be useful to buy a fridge thermometer to check the temperature in your fridge. The coldest part should be around 3°C.

Freezers and fridge-freezers

There are two main types of freezer: upright freezers (which may be full-height or worktop-height) and chest freezers, which have a top-opening lid. Chest freezers obviously take up more floor space, but have the advantage of being able to store larger items. This can be difficult in an upright freezer, many of which have fixed shelves.

The temperature inside the freezer compartment should be between –18°C and –15°C. Higher temperatures are acceptable for shorter periods of time (see table below).

Fridge-freezers may be 'type I' or 'type II'. The type I variety has a single thermostat; the type II has two thermostats. This means the temperature of both compartments can be set independently, so you can keep the fridge operating when defrosting the freezer.

Freezer star ratings

The star ratings of one to four seen on refrigeration products relate to the temperature of the appliance. The stars indicate how long frozen food can be stored and whether fresh food can be frozen down (see the table below). Always check the instructions on the packet of food for specific guidance.

Star rating	Temperature	Storage period
****	–18°C or colder	3 to 12 months. Only four-star units can freeze down fresh food from room temperature
***	–18°C	3 to 12 months. Not suitable for freezing down fresh foods
**	–12°C	Up to one month (pre-frozen foods)
*	–6°C	One week (pre-frozen foods)

All stand-alone freezers, and the freezer sections of two-door fridge-freezers, have a four-star rating. Most freezer boxes in standard fridges are rated one-, two- or three-star.

You should regularly defrost your freezer to maximise energy efficiency. The recommended interval is every six months, although you may have to defrost it more regularly if it is an older appliance, as it will be working harder to maintain core temperature.

Freezers out in the cold

Freezers and fridge-freezers have a 'climate class', which indicates the room temperature at which the appliance is designed to operate, as follows.

> N class: 16–32°C
> SN class: no lower than 10°C
> ST class: 18–38°C
> T class: 18–43°C

Below the recommended minimum temperature, the appliance's cooling system may not be fully effective. If the ambient temperature falls below zero, there is a risk that the appliance could cease to function.

Keeping a freezer in an unheated room such as a garage, therefore, is not recommended. In practice, however, there is often no alternative since many homes are too small to keep such a large appliance anywhere else. (At the point of purchase, the sales assistant should ask where you are likely to be keeping the appliance.)

If you do need to house your freezer in an unheated room, it is a good idea to try to keep a 'history' of the freezer's internal temperatures. You can use an electronic 'max/min' thermometer near the lid, to warn you if the internal temperature has become too warm.

Getting the best from your fridge or freezer

- Make sure your fridge and freezer are no more than three-quarters full, as space is needed around the food for air to circulate, especially in frost-free freezers.
- Don't allow dust and fluff to build up on the condenser coils at the back of your fridge. This can cause up to 30 per cent energy loss if unattended to.
- Regularly check the temperature inside the refrigerator compartment and the freezer. If the temperature is colder than the minimum recommended on page 94, then energy is being wasted and the temperature control needs to be adjusted. Consider placing a fridge/freezer thermometer in your fridge to check that these temperatures are maintained.
- Test the door seal and check that it is tight. If there is an air leak, it will waste energy and you will have to defrost the appliance more frequently. Check that the door shuts easily and does not swing open after you have closed it.

Cookers and microwaves

According to the Market Transformation Programme (see page 92), cooking accounts for 12 per cent of electricity used in our homes and 2.5 per cent of gas. For those who use electric cookers alone, cooking will account for almost a quarter of all electricity used.

Gas is the obvious choice if you have a mains supply. It is cheaper than electricity and is also responsible for less carbon dioxide emissions. Most people find gas cookers easier to control than electric ones. Note that, unlike electric cooking, gas cooking is 'moist', meaning that it gives off water vapour as it burns. This is something to be aware of in terms of the risks of condensation (see Chapter 3).

Range cookers, such as Agas or Rayburns, can be powered by solid fuel or oil (you can also get gas or electric Agas), and some will heat your water and provide central heating as well. These cookers were designed on energy-efficient principles. They have the advantage of providing a heat source in the kitchen, and the heat is instantly available for cooking – so there is none wasted in warming up the oven. Further information is available from the Solid Fuel Association★.

Electric cookers

Electric cookers include conventional, fan-assisted and multi-function models. Conventional ovens use convection heat, which means that the heat is not evenly distributed. They are not ideal for batch baking (cooking on several levels), although they are good for making bread, pastry and for long, slow cooking. On the other hand, fan-assisted cooking is ideal for batch baking as heat is distributed evenly by circulating hot air continuously around the oven. Fan-assisted ovens are much faster at heating up and cook faster at lower temperatures.

Multifunction ovens offer several cooking options – conventional, fan-assisted and grill – in one unit.

You can choose from a variety of hobs on electric ovens.

- **Radiant rings** are the cheapest option. These are generally slower to heat up and cool down than other hob types.
- **Sealed plate hobs**, like radiant rings, are slow to heat up and cool down. The plates have red spots, which are designed to heat up faster, and the fact that they are sealed makes them easier to clean than radiant rings.
- **Ceramic hobs** consist of radiant heating elements, often combined with halogen or semi-halogen elements, under heat-resistant glass.
- **Halogen** units are faster than radiant rings and easy to control. Many units have 'hob hot' lights which indicate that the hob is still hot even though the rings themselves look cool. The lights stay on until the temperature falls to a safe level, which is particularly useful on ceramic hobs.

Gas cookers

Many people choose gas hobs because of the instant, controllable heat. A typical hob might offer two normal burners, a simmer burner and a rapid boil burner. You can ignite the hob by hand, or through electric ignition, which uses the mains electricity to provide a spark to ignite the gas (this is the more common option these days).

With the standard type of gas grill (a poker or fret grill), flames can be seen coming out of a burner. This means that the heat will be uneven. Surface-combustion type grills sandwich the flame between two pieces of fine wire mesh or gauze, which causes the grill to heat evenly. Ceramic grills have gas burners behind a sheet of ceramic glass in the oven roof, allowing more even heat distribution and higher temperatures.

Getting the best from your cooker

- When boiling vegetables, use just enough water to cover the food. Put a lid on the saucepan and turn the controls down to simmer once it has come to the boil.
- Try cooking more than one type of vegetable in the same saucepan, or use a stacked system to steam different types of vegetables.
- Use the grill for things like chops, as this is more economical than the oven. For making toast, a toaster is more economical than the grill.
- Before heating the oven, remove any shelves, baking trays, etc. that aren't being used, as they will absorb heat.
- Modern, fan-assisted ovens need very little pre-heating.
- Try using a pressure cooker, which cooks food faster than a saucepan on one ring.

Microwave ovens

Using a microwave is an easy way to cut down on energy consumption. A microwave oven uses microwave energy, as opposed to radiant heat as in a cooker. This means food can be cooked at the touch of a button rather than having to wait for a conventional oven to heat up. Typical electricity consumption is 1,100W to 1,500W, which is less than half the amount used by a conventional oven. And as microwave energy cooks much faster than radiant heat, overall cooking times are often half that of conventional cooking, or even less.

The most popular type of microwave oven defrosts and reheats food and drink as well as cooking. To brown food, you need a microwave with a grill. The grill can be used on its own or to finish off dishes such as macaroni cheese or shepherd's pie where a browned top is desired. Grills are normally radiant or quartz, with quartz the more powerful (around 1,300W).

Combination models, which include a convection oven, are also available. These use radiant elements and a fan to heat the oven cavity. They often have two shelf positions and a larger capacity.

Power levels range from 800W to 1,000W, with grills from 1,000W to 1,300W. Most models give the user a choice of power levels depending on the type of food, liquid or function required.

Washing machines

Washing machines use energy to power the motor, and to heat and pump the water. Most machines on the market heat the water within the machine by means of electricity. This accounts for some 90 per cent of the energy consumed. Machines that use domestic gas-heated water ('hot fill') are more energy efficient.

Washing machine programmes dictate the temperature, water level, wash rhythm cycling, wash speed and spin speed. This will vary according to the type of clothes being washed. Many washing machines now have energy-saving or 'half-load' programmes, which use less water. (See Chapter 5 for more about saving water.)

Washing machines generally take 5kg loads, though some take 3.5kg or as much as 10kg. Larger machines are, unsurprisingly, less energy-efficient than smaller models, unless used with a full load.

When buying a washing machine, consult the EU Energy Label (see page 89). The three most important things to look for are energy efficiency, washing performance and spin-drying efficiency. An 'A' rating is the best, while a 'triple-A' rating indicates that the machine is a top performer in all areas, according to the manufacturer.

Under the 'Washright' scheme launched in 1998, European soap and detergent manufacturers have agreed to improve the biodegradability of their products and use less packaging, as well as educating consumers to use the correct amount of detergent.

Getting the best from your washing machine

- Don't under- or over-fill your machine. Under-loading can cause clothes to gather on one side of the drum and make the load unbalanced, which may result in banging on the final spin. However, if too many clothes are loaded into the drum, they will form an immovable lump, and will not have any space to move when the drum rotates. Clothes need to be agitated in order to be properly cleaned.

- Try to use the recommended amount of detergent for the type of fabric and the level of soiling. Many of us use far too much detergent.

- Residual suds are usually an indication that you are using too much detergent for the amount or type of clothes that you are washing. Try reducing the amount of detergent by half.

- Pre-treat or soak stains. This may enable you to use a lower temperature or shorter cycle when you come to wash the soiled clothes. (See *Which? Way to Clean It* from Which? Books* for advice on stain removal.)

- Most laundry loads can be washed in warm water (40°C). Washing clothes at 40°C instead of 60°C uses a third less electricity.

- Use hot water only when essential and depending on the type of soil. For a 'maintenance wash' (which should be run occasionally to clean the machine), select 90°C.

- Follow the manufacturer's instructions so that you know which are the most energy-efficient programmes to use.

Warning

Those with sensitive skins need to be careful when selecting energy-efficient washing machines as water consumption is often decreased. Instead you could buy a machine with a 'deep' rinse option or one that allows you to add extra rinses during the wash cycle.

Tumble-driers

As about 95 per cent of the energy used by tumble-driers is for heating, they are not the most energy-efficient of appliances. Energy-saving alternatives are to dry washing outdoors or indoors over radiators. However, according to a *Which?* survey in November 1997, one in three households use their drier all year round. Typically, driers are used four times a week in fine weather and six times a week when it is raining.

All tumble-driers work on the same principle – hot air is passed into a rotating drum to dry the clothes. Some models use gas to heat the air while using electricity to turn the drum. Gas tumble-driers cost a little more to buy than standard electric machines. They need professional fitting and regular inspections. However, they can be three times cheaper to run than electric models, and are responsible for less greenhouse gas emissions. Unfortunately, *Which?* found that they were not as reliable as many electric driers, so any savings in drying costs should be balanced against the inconvenience and costs of repairs.

Washer-driers

Washer-driers are hybrid machines – they both wash and dry. *Which?* recommends them only if you have no other option, as the ones tested for an article in February 1998 cost a lot to run and did not perform particularly well. Some manufacturers provide stacking kits so that you can put a tumble-drier safely on top of a washing machine if space is tight, and this may be a better solution than a combined washer-drier.

Dishwashers

Whether or not you regard a dishwasher as a luxury, it does save time and keep the kitchen tidy – especially if you have a large family or entertain frequently. Many of the models tested by *Which?* used little more than two washing-up bowls of water to clean a full load, so dishwashers are not quite the energy hogs they may first appear.

A typical wash cycle uses about 1.5kWh worth of electricity and 15–20 litres of water. 'Efficient' or 'eco-wash' cycles can be selected. The drawback is that some are quite long (up to three hours in some cases), but if you turn on the machine after your last meal at night the crockery will be ready for use the next morning.

Energy labels for dishwashers are similar to those for washing machines and tumble-driers, allowing consumers to compare wash performance, energy rating and drying efficiency (see page 89). Some 'triple-A'-rated machines are found at the top of the range. The water consumption indicator is an important consideration if you have a water meter (see Chapter 5). Good retailers should be able to help you work out the annual water and electricity costs, if unit costs in their area are known.

Smaller dishwashers may not save energy

Beware of false economy if you buy a slimline model (typically eight place settings). These use more energy per place setting, so are only cheaper if you have less crockery to wash. If space is an issue, however, your choice will be limited.

Brown goods

Owing to digital innovation and the number of new devices (computers, fax and answering machines, larger and digital TVs, cordless phones, etc.) that have entered our homes, we are consuming more power than ever before. These gadgets draw power when in use, of course, but that is only part of the story. More and more of our entertainment and communications equipment use power when they are not being used, and it is this hidden power consumption that is the problem.

Much of our electronic equipment is never switched off, it just goes into a 'standby mode'. Some gadgets, such as TVs or hi-fi systems, draw a small amount of power when they are in this standby mode, so they can 'wake up' when you point a remote control at them. Other items, such as VCRs, have to be in a permanent standby mode in order to keep their clocks going and to record programmes you have set up in advance. Digital TV set-top boxes and personal video recorders are permanently on so the broadcasters can access them remotely to update the electronic programme guides and check billing status. Many items such as cordless phones and answering machines are permanently powered up in order to work or to keep their batteries charged up.

In addition to all this, some products draw standby power for no reason at all – mobile phone chargers, for example, are often left plugged in to the mains even when they are not being used. Other wall-mounted power supplies, such as those used for portable radios or games machines, are always drawing a small amount of power – just feel them, if they are warm, they are using power.

It is true that in many cases we are talking about very small amounts of standby power – perhaps fewer than 3 watts per item – but the problem is that it all adds up. Of course, the effect it has on your electricity bill is quite small too: maybe £11 per year for the average household. When multiplied by the 25 million households in the UK, however, that adds up to a lot – the wasted consumption is actually the equivalent of the full output of two new power stations.

Excessive standby power taken by idle wall adapters, TVs and VCRs is an avoidable waste of energy. New power-supply technologies, coupled with government legislation or voluntary agreements with industry, are significantly reducing this waste. However, the rapid development and take-up of digital television reception platforms will soon compromise any savings made. It is estimated that by 2005 digital TV reception equipment will in effect double the amount of electricity used by electronic equipment in the home. The average household will be using more electricity for electronic equipment than for fridges and freezers combined.

Tips for reducing hi-tech power consumption

- Get into the habit of switching off (or at least to standby) hi-fi and video equipment which is not being used.
- Switch off the battery chargers for your mobile phone or personal stereo when not in use.
- Configure your computer so it automatically goes into standby mode and blanks the screen when not being used.

Escalating power consumption

A house with three TVs, a VCR, a digital set-top box and a home cinema system with built-in DVD player (sold in millions in high-street electronics stores in 2002) uses more electricity running these products than for the fridge and freezer.

Further reading and useful websites

Energy Inform. *The Energy Advice Handbook* (3rd ed). 2003

www.energy-plus.org Europe-wide resource on energy-efficient cold appliances

www.icer.org.uk Recyclers' Directory (includes companies which recycle brown goods)

www.mtprog.com Market Transformation Programme (MTP) – a strategic policy unit run by Defra

www.retra.co.uk Electrical and electronic retailers' trade association

www.ukepic.com The MTP's UK Environmental Product Information Consortium

Chapter 5

Water

Modern living has led to an increasing demand for water. Washing machines and dishwashers, bathing and showering, car washing, garden watering and swimming pools all put stress on the natural supply of water. This is exacerbated in summer months by increased demand at a time of low rainfall. As a result, in some parts of the UK we are now seriously interfering with the environment as we create new reservoirs and lay new pipework. In some areas, groundwater supplies – subterranean caches in the soil and rock – are being depleted. Leakage from water company mains adds to the problem and, in some cases, is as high as 25 per cent of supply.

Saving water is not an obvious necessity since, unlike fossil fuels, it is a resource that is constantly replenished. However, if demand continues to grow there will be serious cost and environmental implications as new and more expensive sources of water are pressed into use. Contamination of groundwater, rivers and lakes is likely to become more of an issue. Furthermore – as discussed in Chapter 1 – climate change is expected to lead to greater variability of rainfall, and we will have less water in the summer when demand is highest. This could put great stress on our water environment – for example, wildlife in rivers and streams. It is therefore essential that we use water wisely.

Water supply and demand

Water conservation is important in light of these environmental considerations, but we have been slow to change our habits. In fact, in the last 20 years the amount of water we use in our homes has increased by over 25 per cent. The Centre for Alternative Technology (CAT)★ suggests that wastefulness is linked to the lack of an economic imperative to save water – most of us pay fixed rates for our water, regardless of how much we use. By contrast, customers with a water meter consume 10 to 20 per cent less on average. See page 110 for more about water meters. Even if you don't fit a meter, you can still take steps to save water.

Most of us use around 150 litres of water per day, but CAT estimates that 80 litres per person per day is a reasonable target for overall sustainability in ordinary homes. To find out how much water you use in a typical day, you can complete a home 'water audit' (see box).

Water audit

Simply write down how often you carry out the following activities in a week, add up the amount of water used, and divide by seven.

Activity	Litres used
Bath	80
Shower	35
Power shower	80
Toilet flushing	6–9
Clean teeth/wash hands and face (under a running tap)	8
Cooking and food preparation (per person)	15
Washing up	12
Washing machine load	65
Dishwasher load	25
Waste disposal unit	16
Hose usage in garden or washing car (10 minutes' use)	150

You may be surprised at how much water you consume. However, it is possible to become more efficient and reduce this amount.

Saving water in the home may involve a little extra time and effort and changing some of our habits, but it is not particularly difficult or costly. For example, simply turning off the tap when you clean your teeth will save around eight litres of water a minute. Putting a water-saving device in your cistern can save around a litre of water for every flush.

Plumbing maintenance

A dripping tap can waste 16 litres of water a day – over a bathful a week – and should be repaired as soon as possible. Taps fitted with washers should need no more than gentle finger pressure to turn off – if you have to use force, it is a sign that the washer is on the way out and will need replacing soon.

Keep an eye on your plumbing pipework for water loss as well. Pipes may leak if damaged by an impact or freezing temperatures.

Plumbing tips

- Maintain plumbing pipes and fittings to prevent leaks.
- Check all valves are working properly.
- Insulate cold-water tanks and all pipes in exposed areas (lofts, under floors and outbuildings) to prevent them from freezing. If a frozen pipe bursts, it can waste a lot of water (see Chapter 3 for details of pipe and tank insulation).
- Report leaks in the water company's service pipes as soon as possible.
- Know where the main stopvalve is – and how to turn it off – in case of emergency.

For more details and an explanation of how to carry out plumbing jobs around the house, see *The Which? Book of Plumbing and Central Heating.*

Saving water

In the bathroom

The main ways of saving water in the bathroom are to reduce the amount of water used for flushing the toilet, to take showers instead of baths and to turn off the taps when washing and cleaning your teeth.

Toilet flushing

Flushing the toilet accounts for 30 per cent of domestic water use on average, and provides considerable scope for water saving. The simplest measure you can take is to put something into the cistern (the container above the toilet bowl) to reduce the amount of water it holds, and thus the amount used per flush. You could use a normal house brick, but a special device (such as a 'Hippo') may be provided free by your water company. The Doing Your Bit campaign, run by Defra★, also offers free water-saving devices.

If this is not possible (perhaps because it interferes with the ball-valve mechanism), you might consider replacing the existing toilet cistern with one of a smaller capacity. Many older cisterns have a capacity of 9 litres or 7.5 litres; cisterns made today have a maximum flush of 6 litres to meet water regulations.

If possible, try not to use too many caustic toilet bowl cleaners or, at least, try to use them less frequently, as some of these products can damage plastic and rubber toilet parts, which can, in turn, lead to leaks. Milder, 'green' products are available. If you really can't give up the household bleach then try to dilute it as much as possible. Toilets seldom need the high concentration of cleaning products we throw down them as these are really designed for removal of built-up stains – or, in the case of foaming or fizzing tablets – heavy limescale deposits.

Dual-flush toilets

Modern dual-flush toilets provide two flush options – a full flush that uses 6 litres of water, and a partial flush that uses 4 litres.

Waterless toilets

Although these are not a likely option for the ordinary house and require practice to use, they are gradually gaining favour, particularly in the United States and Scandinavia. Several models are available, with composting and incinerator toilets being the most commonly used. Although these products use no water at all and are therefore excellent in terms of water efficiency measures, they are expensive and require maintenance. Companies dealing in these types of toilet include Elemental Solutions★ and Construction Resources★.

Baths and showers

The average five-minute shower uses around 30 litres of water (or 6 litres per minute), compared with around 80 litres for a bath, so it makes sense to switch to showering – watch out if you have a power shower, though (see box). Showers also save energy, as your hot water heater has less work to do. If you don't want to give up wallowing in the bath, try replacing one bath each week with a shower.

To conserve water in the shower, turn off the water when soaping yourself or shampooing your hair.

The power shower trap

The increasingly popular 'power showers' use large amounts of water. Flow rates can be as high as 12 to 15 litres a minute – especially if the shower is fitted with side body jets. It's tempting to stay under power showers for longer, perhaps using *more* water than running a bath! To counteract this, take shorter showers (say, from three to five minutes).

When having a bath, you can save water and energy in the following ways:

- Only fill the bath as much as you need – and don't fill it so much that water pours through the overflow outlet when you get in.
- Check the temperature of the water as you fill the bath. This will save your having to fill the bath with cold water to achieve the right temperature. It will also save the energy used to heat the excess hot water.
- Make sure that your bath plug doesn't leak. Replace the plug or plug washer if necessary.
- Save your bathwater and use it in the garden (see Chapter 6).

In the kitchen

Washing machines and dishwashers use lots of water – 65 litres per load and 25 litres per load respectively – so you should operate them only when you have enough for a full load. Alternatively use the half-load button or eco-setting (though note this may save energy but involve increased water use). When buying a new appliance, remember to look at the energy label to check its water consumption (see Chapter 4).

You can save water in the kitchen in other ways too:

- wait until you have a full bowl of dishes before washing up
- don't wash fruit or vegetables under running water – fill a bowl instead

- keep a bottle of tap water in the fridge so you can have a drink without having to run the tap until it gets cold.

Water meters

The majority of householders (77 per cent) are on an unmeasured charge, which means that they pay a set amount for their water and sewerage services, regardless of how much they use. This charge is based on the old rateable value of the house. The other 23 per cent of householders have a water meter. Water meters are compulsory for new homes (those built after 1990, when the rateable value was scrapped), and your water supplier has the right to install a meter in your home if you use a large amount of water for non-essential purposes – for example, if you have a swimming pool or automatic garden watering system.

Many people would be better off paying for the actual amount of water they use. Every household in England, Wales and Scotland has the right to request a free water meter. Once it is installed, you generally pay a standing charge and then a certain amount for each cubic metre (1,000 litres) used. A water company may refuse to fit a meter if it would be unreasonably expensive or impractical to do so – for example, if plumbing alterations would be necessary. But if you pay for this work then your supplier should fit the meter for free. If it is impossible to fit a meter (for example, if you live in a block of flats) your supplier should instead offer you the right to pay an 'assessed charge'. This is usually based on what other metered customers in your area pay, or on an estimate of your usage.

In Northern Ireland, unlike other parts of the UK, householders don't have to pay for their water and sewerage. These services are provided by the Water Service and are funded from the Northern Ireland budget and charges to the non-domestic sector. The government recently announced plans to consider introducing domestic water charges, but any decision would be subject to a full public consultation.

Choosing whether to install a water meter

If you have the choice between the unmeasured charge or a meter, you can do some sums to work out which is likely to be cheaper. As a rule, if you live in a property with a high rateable value and don't use much water, you will be better off with a meter. On the other hand, if your home has a low rateable value and you use quite a lot of water, then you may be better off on unmeasured charges. You may choose to get a meter despite the expense if the environment is a concern.

Ask your water company for a water-use calculator to help you compare what you would pay with metered and unmeasured charges (or consult a website such as www.buy.co.uk for an on-line comparison). Consider your water use carefully and weigh up the pros and cons of metering before you decide.

If you do install a meter, and you don't use much water, you will see the difference in your bills. You can monitor your water use (provided the meter is accessible) and, if the meter has been installed at your request, you have a year to switch back to unmetered charging.

Consumers' Association research has shown that a meter alone doesn't normally encourage people to reduce their water consumption – advice on using water efficiently is also essential.

Reading a water meter

Indoor water meters are usually located on the cold water supply pipe, close to where it enters the property. Externally fitted meters are housed in a meter chamber outside the property. To take a meter reading you need to lift the small metal cover of the meter chamber and remove the polystyrene cover over the meter face.

Although meters vary in size, reading the meter is easy. Simply look at the dial on your meter and record the number of cubic metres it is registering. This is shown by the white numbers on the black dials (ignore the numbers in red).

Water quality and composition

Hard and soft water

If you live in a hard water area, scaling can often occur as 'fur' builds up around heating elements (look in your kettle, for example). This, in turn, can affect the performance of certain appliances. De-scaling products can be used to remove any scale caused by hard water deposits, but a 'greener' alternative is to use distilled white vinegar to remove limescale build-up in kettles and toilets. However, you may need to repeat the process several times to get the desired result.

Lower temperatures equal less scale

Keeping your hot water at 60°C (140°F) or below, will provide an adequate temperature for bathing and washing clothes, and will also help prevent a lot of scale (though not on kettle elements, immersion heaters or the elements of electric showers).

In soft water areas, limescale may not build up so quickly, but soap and detergents may produce foam more easily. This means that you will probably not need to use quite as much washing-up liquid for your dishes or washing powder in your laundry. (In fact, regardless of whether we live in a soft or hard water area, most of us use far too much detergent for the amount of soiling that needs to be removed.) One option, for those who live in a hard water area but would prefer softened water, is to install a water softener. For further information contact your water company, which should be able to give you further advice on installation. However, if you decide to install a softener you must maintain a supply of hard water from the mains to the kitchen cold water tap for cooking and drinking.

Pollutants

Water consciousness is not just about saving water, but also about minimising pollution. When water leaves our homes it is generally contaminated with organic waste (such as urine, faeces, paper and food waste) as well as a variety of household chemicals– used to clean our homes and in our domestic appliances.

Many household cleaning products contain bleach and chemical agents, which can find their way into rivers. Washing powders, for instance, contain phosphates which, when released into our lakes and rivers, cause pollution and lead to the death of fish and other organisms. A simple way to reduce the harm chemicals do to water supplies is to use only as much as you need. In terms of the environment, the main consideration is the biodegradability of certain chemicals. There are now 'greener' alternatives to most types of washing powder or domestic cleaning products.

When we put anything more than organic waste or paper down the toilet, it has to be physically removed before the water can be recycled into our rivers. Materials such as plastic, tampons and sanitary towels, disposable nappies, cotton buds, condoms and cigarettes should, therefore, all be put in the bin instead. See Chapter 7 for more about the responsible disposal of these products.

Your water supply

In England and Wales, water and sewerage services are provided by a number of different local water companies. The Office of Water Services (OFWAT)* is the economic regulator of the water and sewerage industry, so is responsible for ensuring quality of service and fair pricing. WaterVoice* is the water consumers' watchdog.

Several organisations work to safeguard water standards. The Environment Agency* investigates the pollution of rivers and our water supply, while the Drinking Water Inspectorate* regularly checks that the water companies supply water that is safe to drink and meets the standards set in The Water Supply (Water Quality) Regulations 2000.

The water service provider in Scotland is Scottish Water*, and in Northern Ireland it is the Water Service*.

Water companies have special legal powers under the Water Regulations to protect their supplies against contamination, waste, undue consumption and misuse. The Regulations guard against contamination by preventing backflow, back-siphonage or inter-connection of water from other sources. Water UK* represents the interests of water suppliers throughout the UK, at both national and European level.

Taste and appearance of your water

Normally your water supply should look clear and bright with no visible particles, clouding or colour changes, but on rare occasions its appearance could be different. If you are concerned about your water supply's appearance, do not drink it and contact your supplier.

The following are the most common problems people encounter.

- **White or cloudy water**   Air in the water is the most likely cause. Air may be present in the mains, or it may be due to a faulty tap.

- **Yellow, orange or brown or black water**   The most common cause is the disturbance of iron deposits in the mains. This can be caused by a burst water main. Alternatively, it might be rust if you have an old galvanised cold water storage cistern. Check whether the discolouration originates from the mains (cold water kitchen tap) or storage cistern (bathroom tap).
- **Blue or blue/green water**   Caused by new or deteriorating copper pipes within your own plumbing system.
- **White particles**   These are caused by boiling hard water, and are often visible as scale in kettles.

Chlorine taste

Most water supplies contain a small amount of chlorine to minimise harmful bacteria and ordinarily this should not present any problems with the taste or smell of your supply. Occasionally, however, water companies may increase the amount of chlorine they add in order to maintain the standard of protection needed for human consumption.

If you can taste or smell chlorine in your drinking water, try keeping a jug of fresh tap water in your fridge for a few hours as this can help reduce the chlorine taste. You can buy water jugs that take replaceable filter cartridges to purify your tap water, but if you choose this option the water should be used within 24 hours (store it in the fridge) or it can deteriorate.

You can, if you prefer, install a permanent activated carbon filter on the cold water feed to the kitchen sink, connected to its own tap. This will provide chlorine-free water for you to drink or to cook with, but you must change the filter regularly.

Possible pollutants

Nitrates

Since most of our water is taken from rivers and streams, there is an almost unavoidable risk of nitrate fertiliser contamination. Nitrate fertilisers used in agriculture can run off into streams and, more significantly, seep into groundwater when more is applied than can be taken up by crops.

Pesticides

In addition to nitrates, a large proportion of pesticides are used in agriculture to kill insects and weeds. These too can run off into rivers and groundwater but are normally well below accepted danger levels.

Lead

It is now widely accepted that lead is a toxic substance and that we should try to minimise our intake. When water leaves the water companies' treatment works there is very little lead in it, so any significant level tends to originate from old supply pipes and in homes through the use of lead pipes or the solder in old capillary joints linking copper pipework.

Lead piping is only present in homes built before 1960. You can tell if you have lead piping in your home because the pipes are a dull grey colour, and when scratched reveal a bright silver sheen. If you do have lead pipes the level of lead in your water will vary. Higher levels tend to be found when water has been lying in the pipes for a while – for instance, first thing in the morning.

To limit the levels of lead in your water, try running the tap for a couple of seconds before you drink it, so that you are drawing fresh water from the mains. This is particularly important in soft water areas since soft water dissolves lead more readily than hard water. Alternatively, if you have a soft water supply, it may be worth considering replacing all lead pipework that supplies drinking water taps in your home. Modern capillary joints do not contain lead, so can be used to replace joints on drinking water pipes. Your water company should be able to give you advice on replacing lead pipework, and some local authorities offer grants to help you with the cost of replacing lead piping.

Further reading and useful websites

Borer, P. et al. *The Whole House Book*. Centre for Alternative Technology, 1998

Campbell, S. *The Home Water Supply*. Storey Books, 2000

Holloway, D. *The Which? Book of Plumbing and Central Heating*. Which? Books, 2000

Stauffer, J. *The Water Crisis*. Earthscan, 1998

www.buy.co.uk To compare utilities suppliers and work out the likely cost of metered water

www.watervoice.org.uk Answers to common questions and consumer advice about your water supply

Chapter 6

Conservation in the garden

The environmental and energy-saving benefits of saving water were discussed in Chapter 5. Conserving water is particularly important in the garden, which can account for a high proportion of domestic water use in summer. This chapter explains how to conserve and

---

Gardening in the global greenhouse

According to a 2002 report by the National Trust* and the Royal Horticultural Society*, some of the best-loved features of our gardens are under threat as a result of the impact of global climate change (see Chapter 1). The long-term survival of the UK's famous historic public gardens and parks could be at risk.

The report claims that within the next 50 to 80 years, the quintessential 'English country garden' could become increasingly difficult and costly to maintain, and that some traditional garden features may have to be replaced by new ones more suited to changing environmental conditions.

Warmer, wetter winter weather will increase the susceptibility of plants to diseases. Heavier winter rainfall may increase instances of erosion and flooding. Peak demand for water in the garden will occur when it is least available – for example, during summer droughts and in the more densely populated south-east of England, where groundwater reserves are lowest. Managing rainwater run-off and water conservation measures will, therefore, become increasingly essential.

Fortunately, domestic gardeners are in a good position to adapt to climate change. Most gardens could store much more water than they do at present, and careful soil management can increase the earth's moisture-holding properties.

---

recycle water and adapt your garden to weather the 'greenhouse effect'. It also provides tips on recycling and composting, and makes some 'green' gardening suggestions that will help you conserve the natural environment.

Reducing water use in the garden

You might be surprised at how much water your garden soaks up. In summer, if no rain fell:

- a 3×4m vegetable patch and a small greenhouse containing two growbags of tomatoes and one grow-bag each of cucumbers, aubergines and peppers would need around 7,500 litres (equivalent to 94 baths)
- a 5×10m lawn would need about 28,000 litres to keep it green and lush – enough water to keep a family of four going for 58 days
- six hanging baskets and 12 containers would need around 2,000 litres. That's more than 250 toilet flushes' worth.

Reducing water use in the garden makes sense for many reasons. It lessens the environmental impact of water extraction, and improves your garden's resilience (plants that can only survive on water handouts demonstrate poor performance and increased susceptibility to pests and diseases in times of water shortage). It also saves money if you have a water meter, and reduces the amount of work – many water-saving measures are also labour-saving.

There are many ways to save water – and time – in your garden while still keeping it blooming. You can make adaptations to your garden so that it needs less moisture, water your plants more efficiently or set up automated watering devices.

Creating a water-saving garden

Adopting a water-saving approach in the garden will not only save you time and money, it will also help your garden to withstand drier summer conditions – which may increase as a result of global warming. This means watering what you've got more efficiently and reducing your garden's water demands.

When thinking about making your garden more water-conscious, you will need to consider the soil type, aspect, style of planting and facilities available. For example, if your garden is exposed to full sun, subjected to high winds or has a very free-draining soil, the likelihood of its suffering from drought is higher. If, on the other hand, it is sheltered from both wind and sun and has a heavy, water-retaining soil, its water demands will be much less.

Whatever type of garden you have, follow these general rules to conserve water:

- group moisture-loving plants together so only one area needs to be kept moist
- choose large, non-porous containers and arrange them in groups
- when planting, dig deeply and add water-holding organic matter as a mulch
- reduce the effect of drying winds by constructing, or growing, windbreaks.

Watering tips

The key to reduced watering is giving your plants the water they need, where and when they really want it. The most important things to focus on are minimising evaporation and getting water directly to the roots of the plants.

Most plants don't need regular watering. You should only need to water newly planted plants, fruit and vegetables at certain stages of development, and plants in containers. For effective watering, follow the advice below.

- Reducing the amount of foliage wetted reduces evaporation and the risk of scorching. Larger plants may act as umbrellas, restricting the area of roots that receive water and leaving under-plantings in the dry, so it is best not to apply water over the tops of plants. Watering devices such as drippers and seep hoses (see page 123) allow water to be applied as close to the ground as possible.
- In warm weather, water plants in the evening – this gives the water a chance to soak down to the roots instead of evaporating in the heat. Remember also that plants generally prefer a good soaking to a quick sip.

- Summer sun can turn the top layer of soil into a solid crust. When this happens, the water runs away before much of it can be absorbed. The answer is to apply water beneath the soil surface using a device such as a soaker hose (see 'Seep and sprinkler hoses', page 123).
- Do not be tempted to give plants a good soaking in very free-draining, sandy soils. The water will drain past the roots before the plant can make use of it. Instead you should water little and often, using drippers and soaker hoses.
- If you use a watering can, use it without a rose and concentrate on watering the plants that really need it, such as leafy vegetables and those in containers.
- If you use a sprinkler attached to a hosepipe, always have some kind of timer fitted between the hosepipe and the garden tap – (see 'Water timers and computers', page 124). At the very least this will turn the water off after a set period: 'forgotten' sprinklers can be a huge waste of water.

Wasting water

Normal garden hoses use 500 to 1,000 litres per hour, depending on water pressure.

Match your watering to the plants' needs

By choosing drought-tolerant plants you can save time as well as water and create some great plant combinations. Plants that do not need much water include lavender, lilacs, tulips, sunflowers, wall-flowers, jasmine, buddleia, holly, broom and crocuses. This is by no means a comprehensive list, however. For more information contact your local gardening centre.

Use mulches

Using mulches is one of the easiest methods of water conservation. A mulch is a water-retaining layer laid on top of the soil. It not only suppresses weeds (which are great water lovers) but also keeps the soil cool, reduces evaporation and soil compaction and can look very attractive. The mulches that are the best weed inhibitors are cocoa shell, finely chipped bark, black plastic sheeting and grass clippings – the last two are most effective at holding moisture in the soil.

Pay attention to your soil

Improving your soil structure is essential to keep plant roots moist, especially in the hottest and driest areas of your garden.

- **Free-draining soils** Add at least a barrowload of organic matter to every 4 sq m and dig in to a depth of 15cm. Every new planting hole should have organic matter added before planting. There are many types of organic matter, but garden compost, spent mushroom compost or well-rotted manure are all ideal.
- **Shallow soils** Dig out planting pits with a pickaxe and fill with improved soil, a good home-made compost or bought multipurpose compost. For shrubs and trees, make the pits at least 60cm deep; for large perennials, 15cm should be adequate.
- **Clay soils** Dig in a 5-cm layer of sharp grit to a depth of 15cm to improve soil structure. Adding the same amount of organic matter will also be beneficial.

Reduce the size of your lawn

Most people want a lawn in their garden. However, it is one of the most demanding components because it needs to be mown and soaks up a lot of water – which makes it grow faster and require cutting again. One significant way in which you can reduce the overall amount of water used is to reduce your lawn's size. Gravel can replace part of the lawn and can be planted with ornamental grasses.

If seeding a new lawn, choose a drought-tolerant mix or shade mix, as these require less watering.

Watering methods

By selecting plants carefully you can have an ornamental garden that requires no watering once established. However, most gardens will have some plants that do need extra water when there has been no rain. You have five choices of watering method:

- watering by hand using a watering can
- watering by hand using a 'hose-end fitting' (a hosepipe fitted with a nozzle or spray gun)

- using a sprinkler attached to a hosepipe run to a tap
- using a seep or sprinkler hose attached to a tap
- using a 'micro irrigation' system with a selection of watering devices attached to small diameter tubing run from a tap.

The last three systems can all be automated so that the watering is done at set times (see 'Water timers and computers', page 124).

Watering by hand
Watering the garden by hand can be extremely time-consuming and hard work – especially if you use a watering can. It can also be very wasteful as some water evaporates before your plants can absorb it. However hand watering may be the only kind you are allowed to do when there is a hosepipe ban in your area.

Hose-end fittings
Fitting a hand-held spray gun, nozzle or lance on to the end of a hosepipe takes a lot of the labour out of garden watering and is not wasteful provided there is an on/off control. Lances allow you to reach right into flowerbeds to get the water to the bottom of plants; special curved lances allow you to water hanging baskets without getting on a step-ladder or taking the basket down.

There is a good selection of nozzles, spray guns and lances available. It is a good idea to get a water stop connector. This shuts off the water supply when a fitting is removed, allowing you to change fittings easily without needing to go back to the tap to turn the water off.

Sprinklers
Sprinklers are convenient and time-saving, but are the worst culprits for wasting water. A lot of this waste is due to evaporation or water drifting to where it is not needed. The major offence, however, is leaving sprinklers on for too long – either deliberately or accidentally. A simple water timer (see page 124) will turn the water off after a set period.

Sprinklers water the spaces in between plants, thus encouraging weeds that compete for water once established. Large rotating sprinklers are better if your garden is square-shaped rather than long and narrow, though some water will inevitably be wasted. Oscillating sprinklers can be adjusted to overcome this problem to some extent, and are better suited to narrow gardens.

You need a licence to use a sprinkler in many areas of the UK. Check with your local water company.

Seep and sprinkler hoses

Seep hoses use less water than hosepipes or sprinklers attached to taps. Also known as soaker or 'leaky' hoses, they are made of recycled rubber granules bonded together in such a way that they leak water through their entire length. When turned on, water seeps through the porous sides of the hose and goes direct to the roots of plants. Seep hoses deliver water slowly and hence reduce wasteful run-off, although the amount of water used depends on the pipe length and water pressure. They connect directly to an outside tap, and are ideal for borders. They are usually available from DIY stores or garden centres.

Seep hoses should be 'snaked' through the plants or alongside vegetables – they work best when buried at root level. A light topping of gravel mulch over and around the hose will assist in water efficiency by preventing evaporation and clogging of pores.

It is often too disruptive to dig hoses in and around existing plants, but you may be able to lay one in the ground when planting for the first time. In areas that have already been planted, it is more sensible simply to lay the hose on a loosened soil surface and place a mulch on top. This also enables you to change the position of the hose readily. Fix the depth and spacing of tubing according to the plants' water needs and your soil type. Thirsty plants and sandy soil need shallower tubing, laid more closely.

A seep hose uses only 100 litres of water an hour. You can also fit a timer to your hose so that the water is turned off automatically after a certain time.

A sprinkler hose is a perforated flat hose which produces a gentle sprinkler effect when used upright and a deep soaking action when reversed pointing downwards into the soil. It is best used in straight lines – between rows of vegetables, for example.

Any tap connected to the mains supply must, by law, be fitted with a double-check valve before it is attached to a hose (see box). In some areas it is illegal to connect seep or sprinkler hoses directly to the mains water supply, even if you have a double-check valve. Check with your local water company.

Double-check valves

The Water Regulations require that a double-check valve be fitted to all mains taps which supply a hosepipe. This is to protect the quality of domestic water supply by preventing water from the garden being sucked back into the mains supply (this could happen if there is a drop in pressure). The double-check valve can be fitted in the tap itself, in the pipe leading to the tap or between the hosepipe and the tap – the simplest answer if you do not want to do any extra plumbing.

Micro irrigation systems

A micro irrigation system is a permanent watering system consisting of small-diameter tubing plus watering devices at places where they are needed. The tubing is connected to a garden tap at one end and blanked off at the other; the watering devices are inserted into the tubing as and where they are required.

Various watering devices are available, such as fixed and adjustable drippers, quarter-, half- and full-circle micro jets, tiny sprinklers, and misters (used only in greenhouses) which produce a fine concentrated mist. Spikes are available for mounting any of these devices at a height.

It is possible to buy all the components you need separately and then to design your own micro irrigation system, dividing and joining tubing as required. Or you can buy 'kits' designed specifically for tasks such as patio watering (for containers, tubs and hanging baskets), greenhouse watering (for grow-bags) and watering flower borders or vegetable rows. Complete kits are also available with a water timer included.

Water timers and computers

You can fit a water timer between your garden tap and a hosepipe to control the water flow if you have a sprinkler, seep hose or a micro irrigation system. The simplest form of clockwork water timer can be set to turn the water off a certain period after you have turned it on – typically at any time up to two hours. Electronic (battery-operated) water timers can also be set to turn the water on at the same time each day – even when you are on holiday – and then turn it off after a certain period. Timers are available from about £20.

More elaborate timers – sometimes known as water computers – can be programmed with up to six watering periods a day. They can even be connected to rain sensors and soil moisture sensors to determine watering needs. Water computers can be linked with an automatic water distributor to feed up to six different watering channels, activating one after the other according to a programmed pattern. This is ideal for plants with different water consumption, or if the water flow rate is not sufficient to operate all watering channels at once. A system like this could cost £140 to £150 to buy – perhaps not too much to pay if you have a lot of valuable plants in the garden that could die if they were not watered.

Non-mechanical automated methods

You don't have to buy special equipment to automate your watering – there are also various low-tech methods. One is to create a number of miniature water reservoirs that let water seep slowly into the soil. This allows water to reach the root level directly, and also reduces water wastage through evaporation at the soil surface.

Plastic soft-drinks bottles make large reservoirs which are ideal for established plants – especially deep-rooted ones such as clematis. To utilise a bottle in this way, chop the bottom off (keep it to use as a lid) and insert the bottle carefully into the soil a little way from the plant, so that the narrow end is directed straight to the roots. Alternatively, drill holes in the sides and insert the bottle narrow end-up without cutting off the bottom. Replace the lid (or bottle top) between waterings to keep soil from falling in.

Alternatively, a flexible pipe with holes drilled in can be sunk beyond the perimeter of a new shrub's roots. The pipe acts as a semi-circular reservoir from which water seeps slowly. A piece of washing machine or vacuum cleaner hose is ideal. You could also try using a piece of flexible plastic plumbing pipe.

If you plant in rows, you can dig channels between plants and sink in lengths of guttering with holes drilled in the bottom and end-stops clipped on, so their sides are just above the soil. The advantage of guttering over an open channel is that the sides will not cave in; the disadvantage is that you are restricted to straight lines. These channels can be linked to form lattices for even easier watering. Open channels are likely to need re-digging at intervals, though, or they will become silted up.

Collecting water

With a little ingenuity, you can collect rainwater and waste household water from baths, showers and washing machines for use on your garden.

Rainwater

If you live in a hard water area, your plants are likely to prefer rainwater to tap water. Rainwater can be collected and stored in a water butt – a large container fitted with a tap – or other receptacle. Stored rainwater usually harbours bugs, so may be inadvisable for delicate plants and seedlings.

Water butts can be fitted to garden buildings such as sheds, greenhouses and garages (gutters may need to be fitted first). They are available at garden centres and DIY stores. The standard size is 114 litres, and prices start at about £25. Larger rainwater tanks – up to 700 litres – could cost as much as £200. Some water companies and some local authorities offer special deals on water butts.

You can fit a plastic diverter on to your downpipe to channel water from the roof of your house into a butt or series of linked butts. Some diverters are fitted with a switch that lets you manually divert water from the down pipe to the butt, and they generally have an automatic overflow so that the butt does not spill over. Water diverters cost only a few pounds to buy – some water companies may offer them as a special deal along with water butts.

If you don't like the idea of a butt but still want to collect rainwater, you could use the sort of cheap recycled containers obtainable from places such as soft drinks factories or The Tank Exchange★. If you convert a plastic drum or barrel, make sure it has a lid to prevent unwanted debris accumulating and make it safe for children and animals.

Ensuring rainwater quality

Dirt washed off roofs can contaminate the rainwater you collect. After a dry spell, you could wait for an hour before collecting rainwater in a butt or tank. Keeping guttering free of leaves and grime will also help keep the water clean.

Greywater

'Greywater', or water that has been used in the home for washing and bathing, can be re-used in the garden, providing some simple rules are followed.

- Never re-use water containing bleach, strong detergents, chemicals or household cleaning agents.
- Avoid re-using bath or basin water while a member of the household is ill or using a topical skin treatment.
- Don't use greywater on edible crops.
- Don't pour greywater directly on to plants; water the soil around them.
- Vary where you use greywater in the garden.
- Always allow greywater to cool before re-use.
- Don't store bath and shower water for long or mix it with rainwater – it becomes rancid quickly.
- Don't use very greasy water on your plants; if you garden on clay soil, oily water will tend to clog it.
- Washing machine and dishwasher water are both alkaline, so don't use them on acid-loving plants.
- Don't use water that has been used to wash nappies or clean pets.

Bathroom greywater

Most bath and shower waste water is relatively clean. Collecting water from an upstairs bath, shower or washbasin is not too difficult. One way is to siphon the water out with a hose (using a siphon device available from hardware stores). You could store it in buckets for transportation to the garden. Alternatively, store some of the water in a tank. You could fit a valve-operated branch pipe to the waste pipe leading from your bath and/or shower tray, allowing you to take the water to a temporary holding tank.

Kitchen greywater

A lot of water used in the kitchen (for example, for cooking and washing vegetables) can be re-used in the garden: allow hot water to cool first. Strong detergents are not beneficial to plants, however, so you may prefer not to use the contents of the washing-up bowl, depending on your brand of washing-up liquid (see box overleaf).

Greywater and plant health

Detergents, soap, salt and grease can all cause harm to plants in strong concentrations. However, in most greywater these are too diluted to cause significant damage. An exception are the powerful detergents and cleaners found in household or floor cleaning solutions. These could not only scorch plants, they may also contain boron, which is toxic to plants in excess. Try to avoid re-using waste water containing these ingredients.

If you would like information on how to purify your greywater using sand filters and reed beds, contact the Centre for Alternative Technology (CAT)*. Some products are available which claim to kill the bacteria and prevent odour associated with greywater storage. *Gardening Which?* found that Biotal Refresh Plus, available from most garden centres, killed 85 per cent of bacteria. However, the best thing to do with greywater to prevent bacteria build-up and unpleasant odours is to use it as quickly as possible.

Dealing with waste

In the UK we produce 27 million tonnes of household waste each year, over half of which could be recycled. Recycling in the garden conserves natural resources and offers a creative way to make use of existing items.

Re-using materials is the simplest form of recycling. It may just mean choosing re-usable products over disposables – pump-action sprayers can be refilled, for example, whereas aerosols cannot. Re-use also means finding new uses for waste materials. This is something gardeners excel at, whether it is growing seedlings in yoghurt pots, using old windows to make a coldframe or finding new roles for discarded pallets.

Recycling also involves breaking down products or materials so that they can be made into something else. Composting (see page 132) is a classic example of this, as it makes the nutrients tied up in plant and animal waste available to plants again. Non-organic materials such as plastics can also be recycled.

See Chapter 7 for more details about recycling and waste disposal.

Re-using materials

Re-using materials does not mean that you have to rethink your whole garden. With a little creativity, you can devise some useful accessories and invent a special one-off look that cannot be bought in garden centres.

- Make imaginative use of discarded containers to grow plants – anything that will hold compost and has drainage holes can be used. Schools and community gardens are great sources of inspiration.
- Car tyres can be piled up and filled with compost to grow flowers or vegetables in – they are great for cascades of nasturtiums or easy-access potato crops, and let you grow plants even in a concrete yard.
- Use garden or household objects – from old watering cans to the kitchen sink – to make a water feature (with a small submerged pump that continuously recycles the water from a hidden underground tank). You may be able to find old kitchen and garden objects at car boot sales for a fraction of the price you might pay at a salvage yard.
- Expanded polystyrene packaging can be broken up and used as crocks in containers. If you are putting lots of small plants into large pots you could fill half the container with polystyrene and save compost too, as well as cutting down on weight.
- Use unwanted CDs and audio or video tape to add to your repertoire of bird scarers – move or change them often for maximum effect.
- Grow your own products for re-use. Many shrubs, including buddleia and philadelphus, provide strong, straight shoots which make perfect supports for herbaceous perennials. Hedge prunings can make twiggy sticks, while willow, dogwood or hazel can make tripods to support climbers such as sweet peas, clematis or runner beans, or be woven into cottage garden-style edging to prevent plants from flopping.
- Use several layers of newspaper as a short-term mulch, weighted down with soil; rip it up and mix it into soggy compost to increase aeration; or try making your own biodegradable plant pots with a pot maker from the Organic

Gardening Catalogue, published by the HDRA, The Organic Association★ in association with Chase Organics★.

- Plastic drinks bottles can be cut up to make mini-cloches, slug-protection rings, or funnels and scoops for compost or fertiliser. Larger-sized water bottles make perfect individual cloches, covers for seed trays or water reservoirs.
- Re-use potting compost by adding it to the compost heap, or digging it directly into the soil where you want to add organic matter without adding nutrients. Use it for permanent container plants mixed 50:50 with garden soil. For short-term planting, just revitalise it with a little grit or perlite to improve the structure (a couple of handfuls to a bucketful) plus some slow-release fertiliser.
- Old carpet makes a comfy kneeler – a strip a couple of metres long means you don't have to keep moving it, and allows you to weed with a friend. Old carpet can also be used to smother weeds, to make semi-permanent paths in vegetable plots or to keep maturing compost warm.
- Large plastic paint pots with handles make good storage bins and can be hung up out of the way. You could drill a hole in the base, paint the outside and fill the pot with trailing plants for a cheap alternative to hanging baskets.

Innovation in action

The *Gardening Which?* 'recycled garden' at Capel Manor in north London uses various methods to demonstrate the benefits of recycling. It features large, raised beds made from railway sleepers to form the main planting areas, with telegraph poles used as the basis of a pergola. In addition, the garden has a raised decking area, made of pallets, which houses a collection of recycled containers.

To create a similar look, check the *Yellow Pages* under 'Salvage and reclamation' and 'Pallet and case makers' for your local suppliers. Most salvage yards sell recycled timber. (Note that, as of June 2003, an EU Directive banning the sale to consumers of creosote-treated wood – including railway sleepers – will come into effect.)

Recycling

Gardeners are natural recyclers and you can do a lot to encourage the trend.

- Buy recycled goods. Potting compost, pots, garden fencing, furniture and many other products are now made from recycled materials (see below).
- If you have woody cuttings or small branches to dispose of, don't burn or dump them. Get together with neighbours and hire a shredder for the weekend to turn all the waste into weed-suppressing mulch. The mulch will also help stop the ground drying out and provide cover for useful invertebrates such as slug-munching ground beetles.
- Check out your local recycling facilities. Many areas have schemes to collect and use leftover paint or old tools. Contact the Local Agenda 21 officer at your local council for more information.
- Second-hand timber, bricks and other materials such as reclaimed slate tiles often have more character than new ones. They can also save you money, and can be put to completely new uses in the garden – chimney pots can be used as planters, for example. Try your local salvage yard or roofing supplier for these items.

Recycled products

An increasing number of items that have been manufactured directly from consumer waste are available to buy. Garden products and equipment made from recycled materials include:

- cloches made from recycled plastic
- outdoor clothes, such as fleeces made from recycled plastic bottles
- compost and soil improvers made from bio-solids from sewage treatment works
- compost bins, tumblers, containers and planters made from recycled plastic or reclaimed timbers
- decking, fencing, trellises, gates and other outdoor furniture made from recycled scrap polythene, plastic or reclaimed wood

- plant labels, supports, pots and trays made from recycled plastics
- water-saving equipment such as rain tanks and water butts made from recycled plastics.

A directory of products entitled *Recycled Products for the Garden* is available from *Gardening Which?*★ and the Environment Agency★. It includes advice on community recycling initiatives, educational literature and further sources of information.

In addition you could try the *UK Recycled Products Guide*, published by Waste Watch★, which includes products for industry, office and domestic use. *The Green Directory*★ and the Green Guides★ contain details of suppliers of eco-friendly goods and services.

Composting

If you are serious about recycling, you should invest in a compost bin. As much as 25 per cent of the contents of the average household dustbin is biodegradable, and it is a waste to consign this to a landfill when home-made compost is an excellent mulch and soil improver, and ideal for growing many plants in. Any garden will generate material to make compost, and adding compost will benefit all garden soils. If you add suitable waste from the house, you will also be saving space in the dustbin.

What to compost
Aim to compost all you can. Below we provide a guide to the materials you can – and can't – put in your bin.

Add to compost:
- fruit and vegetable peelings and trimmings
- tea bags and coffee grounds
- shrub prunings, preferably chopped or shredded first
- end-of-season bedding and container plants, and any other discarded plants – but beware of plants infested with vine weevils, and notorious self-seeders such as forget-me-nots
- most weeds (avoid perennial weed roots and any seedheads)
- grass clippings, mixed well with drier material
- anything else of plant or animal origin not listed opposite under 'Avoid'.

Avoid:
- meat or fish (which can encourage pests)
- perennial weed roots and weeds that have flowered
- diseased plants or those infested with soil pests
- man-made materials which won't rot, such as plastics and nylon
- dog and cat droppings – they could contain parasites and diseases
- soot and vacuum cleaner dust, which may contain heavy metals
- thorny prunings – they make handling the compost unpleasant.

Add in small amounts:
- paper (not glossy) and cardboard, if ripped or scrunched-up and well-mixed with the green waste
- natural fibres such as cotton and wool
- sawdust and wood shavings – though these are slow to compost
- conifer clippings – though they can be slow to rot and make the compost acidic.

All plant material will eventually rot down and be recycled back into the soil. A compost bin speeds up the process by providing ideal conditions for the bugs that do the business. You should be able to produce good compost in about three months during summer, slightly longer over winter. Air is essential for efficient composting. For the fastest results, turn the pile of compost at least once a week.

Wait until the compost is well rotted and you are unable to identify any of the original ingredients before digging it into the soil. It should be dark and crumbly and have a pleasant 'earthy' smell. Compost used as a mulch does not need to be quite so well rotted, although it will look more attractive if it is.

If you want to get together with other households and gardeners to start your own local composting scheme, contact The Composting Association*.

Compost bins

Compost bins come in all shapes and sizes. The ideal one for you will depend on how much space you have in your garden and how much waste material it generates. You can make your own compost bin quite easily, which may be the best option if you have a large garden.

Making your own bin

A compost bin can be made of any durable and strong material. Those with good insulating properties are best.

- Don't make the bin too small. The outside surfaces of the materials inside will turn into compost very slowly because conditions are not right. The smallest size that will work well is one about one cubic metre.
- Remember to allow for moisture and air to penetrate, and add a removable side so you can empty the bin – you don't want to have to demolish it to get the compost out. You may also need to turn the compost to increase the aeration.
- Contact with the soil is important, as this allows worms and insects to enter the compost during the final stages. For this reason, some of the compost material should touch the soil, or be fairly close to it. Don't stand the bin on concrete.
- More than one bin will allow you to stagger batches of compost, so that while one is maturing, you can fill the other.

For more information on making your own bin, consult any good gardening manual.

Before buying a bin, check with your local council – many now offer cheap or even free compost bins. Councils, or their contractors, are charged for every tonne of rubbish they tip into

Permaculture

Permaculture is a unique approach to living based on conserving resources and reducing consumption. It is a system of applied design principles for creating sustainable human habitats.

Permaculture designers advocate a radical change to the way in which we grow food, manage land, build homes, use energy and organise communities.

Designers aim to organise a garden and its contents so as to use energy as efficiently as possible and to create a healthy, diverse ecology. This involves the creation of various garden 'zones', used landfill sites. So it is in their interest to encourage householders to reduce waste by composting and recycling.

Organic gardening

Organic gardening exercises long-term care for the environment by avoiding the use of chemicals. In effect, organic gardening mirrors nature's methods of decomposition and renewal.

The aim of organic gardening is to work with nature rather than trying to control it. So natural predators have a large role to play in helping to control pests on your plants and vegetables. You can encourage a wide range of wildlife into the garden by creating favourable habitats such as ponds, meadows and hedgerows.

These measures help contribute to biodiversity (the numbers of different species of plants and animals in the environment). As we continue to destroy natural habitats through developments for housing, manufacturing and new transport systems, re-creating a wildlife-friendly habitat in our gardens becomes increasingly important. Although what we do in our gardens will not necessarily solve all the problems of endangered species, it will help many native species whose habitats are being lost in the wild.

'Green' products

Alternatives to chemical pesticides, herbicides and fungicides are becoming more widely available. Some organic methods of weed

for different activities and plantings. In simple terms, this means putting the areas that need to be visited most often (say, the herb or salad garden) nearest the home, and those that are visited more rarely (say, the orchard) further away.

There are 40 to 50 permaculture gardens in the UK. Details are published in *The Permaculture Plot*, available from the British Permaculture Association*. The Association trains permaculture designers. It can advise on garden opening times – many are not open to the public and you may need to arrange a visit in advance.

and pest control do take more time and effort than a quick chemical fix, but many gardeners prefer to know that they are not harming the environment when they choose to garden organically. One of the best reasons for growing your own vegetables is that you can be absolutely sure how they have been grown and what has been sprayed on them.

Be warned that organic fertilisers are not regulated, and some brands that sound healthy could contain slaughterhouse by-products. If you are not sure where to get good organic fertilisers, the *Organic Gardening Catalogue* (see Chase Organics★ and HDRA★) is a good place to start. Both organisations also supply advice and offer a range of merchandise.

Further reading and useful websites

British Permaculture Association. *The Permaculture Plot.*

Chase Organics and HDRA. *Organic Gardening Catalogue.*

Gardening Which? and the Environment Agency. *Recycled Products for the Garden.* 2002

Gould, J. et al. *Rainwater Catchment Systems for Domestic Supply: Design, Construction and Implementation.* ITDG Publishing, 1999

Green, C. *Gardening Without Water – Creating Beautiful Gardens Using Only Rainwater.* Search Press Ltd, 1999

Hamilton, G. *The Organic Garden Book.* Dorling Kindersley, 2000

Roulac, J. *Backyard Composting.* Green Earth Books, 1999

Stickland, S. *Greenhouses – Natural Fruit and Vegetables All Year Round.* HDRA

Waste Watch. *UK Recycled Products Guide.*

Whitefield, P. *Permaculture In A Nutshell* (2nd ed). Permaculture Resources, 2000

www.livingwater.org.uk Ecological principles applied to a range of water and waste problems for households, agriculture and industry

Chapter 7

Recycling and waste disposal

Each year in the UK we throw out almost 30 million tonnes of household waste – over a third of a tonne per person. There are currently three main options for disposing of this:

- burying it in landfill sites
- burning it in incinerators
- recycling the usable materials.

Landfill

In theory, three-quarters of household waste could be recycled or composted – but in practice almost 80 per cent is sent to landfill. These used to be fairly rudimentary, conveniently sited holes in the ground, where the waste was simply dumped and covered over. It was a cheap way to dispose of rubbish, but poorly thought-out landfill sites have been the cause of environmental concern.

One problem is how to control leachate, a liquid produced when the waste is broken down by bacteria and which mixes with water seeping through the site. On landfills that have impermeable bases and sides, the leachate is collected and disposed of. But on many sites, leachate sinks into the ground. Under natural processes of degradation, this should be broken down, diluted and made harmless. However, some scientists are concerned that certain chemicals in the leachate may not break down safely and can contaminate the underground water system.

Another major problem is landfill gas, a mixture of methane and carbon dioxide produced when the waste breaks down. It should be monitored and vented properly to stop it from building up and possibly causing an explosion.

There is also the more fundamental question of whether we can continue to use land for dumping our waste. We are running out of space for landfill sites, particularly in the south-east of England. By burying almost 80 per cent of all domestic waste, we are using up suitable sites very quickly – mostly by filling them with unsorted domestic waste that contains valuable materials which could be recycled. In an attempt to stem the rising volume of landfill waste, in 1996 the government introduced a Landfill Tax, levied on the amount of rubbish sent to landfills. The Landfill Tax Credit Scheme (LTCS) encourages landfill operators to support a wide range of environmental projects by giving them a 90 per cent tax credit against their contributions to Environmental Bodies (EBs). So as well as deterring landfill, the tax supports recycling and other 'green' initiatives.

Incineration

The second option for waste disposal is to burn it. Municipal

---

The nappy mountain

According to a report by *Ethical Consumer** magazine, more than 90 per cent of parents in the UK opt for disposable nappies. Most of this waste goes straight to landfill – where parts of the nappy will take up to 200 years to decompose. *Which?* has also reported that British parents throw out eight million disposable nappies a day, accounting for four per cent of all household rubbish.

Paper fluff is the largest component of disposable nappies and demand for this material has resulted in the widespread destruction of old growth forests in Scandinavia, Canada and the Baltic states. Paper is particularly hard to break down and, when it does, methane is a likely by-product. Disposable nappies also contain plastics and chemicals derived from non-renewable resources, and as landfill sites do not provide the right conditions for plastics to break down, these materials, along with paper, may persist for decades.

According to one estimate the average baby will use around 5,000 disposable nappies from birth to potty, at a typical cost of £740.

incinerators are owned and operated by local authorities. They burn domestic, commercial and non-hazardous industrial wastes. Some of these produce energy that is then available for district heating or commercial use. Burning waste to make energy sounds like a good solution, but incinerators are themselves a potential environmental hazard.

Incinerator chimneys emit smoke and gases containing a polluting mixture of chemicals and heavy metals. Municipal incinerators also emit dioxins. Some dioxins in sufficient quantities are toxic to humans, but the health risk of exposure to tiny amounts in the environment isn't really known.

Recycling

The greatest potential for reducing the amount of waste that needs to be incinerated or put in landfill sites lies in creating less rubbish in the first place and in recycling far more of our domestic waste.

There are alternatives to disposable nappies. Advice from the Real Nappy Association (RNA)* is to use thin liners inside a terry nappy, which allows for waste to be peeled away and disposed of. Such liners are biodegradable (commonly made of cotton) and are available from most 'real' nappy suppliers. The RNA calculates that savings from using real nappies for a first child alone can amount to £600. Modern re-usable nappies are now available in a variety of styles and materials and are very different from their old square cloth predecessors. When *Which?* asked seven families to try washable nappies for four weeks, five of them said they would continue to use washables in preference to disposables.

Many families choose disposable nappies to save time and to cut down on the extra washing that comes from using re-usable terry nappies. If these are concerns, you could use a nappy washing service instead, which will cost around £9 per week (about the same cost as buying disposable nappies). Your bag of dirty cotton nappies is handed over to a collection service, and a clean supply will be returned to you at the end of the week. Contact the National Association of Nappy Services (NANS) * for further details.

The government has set a target for municipal waste disposal: to recycle or compost at least 25 per cent of household waste by 2005, 30 per cent by 2010 and 33 per cent by 2015. This contrasts with the current figures of 11 per cent in England and 6.9 per cent in Scotland. In Switzerland 52 per cent of household waste is recycled, while the Netherlands, Austria and Germany all achieve levels of around 45 per cent.

Domestic waste contains a surprisingly high proportion of recyclable materials. But in the average dustbin, valuable raw materials like aluminium cans, glass bottles and paper may be mixed up with leftover food, discarded packaging and an increasing amount of plastics. Once recyclable materials are mixed up with the rest of our household waste, it becomes extremely difficult and very expensive to extract the useful resources.

Effective recycling requires careful disposal of each householder's rubbish. You can find out where local recycling facilities are located, and what kinds of materials they take, by contacting your local authority recycling officer. Some local authorities run collection schemes that pick up materials for recycling from your doorstep.

All of the materials below can be recycled.

Make recycling part of your routine

To avoid using extra fuel, try not to make a special journey to the recycling centre. Instead make it a stop-off on a journey you are already making anyway, perhaps during your weekly or monthly shop. Make sure you put items in the right recycling bins.

Glass

Every day, 14 million bottles and jars are buried in landfills. This is extremely wasteful, as glass can be recycled indefinitely. Recycling glass uses less energy than making new glass, reduces pollution and saves valuable materials having to be quarried.

Products that can be made from recycled glass include road surfacing, water filters, paving tiles, kitchen surfaces and, of course, more glass. There are now more than 20,000 bottle banks spread around the UK. Despite this, we still have the lowest recycling rate for glass in Europe. For every tonne of glass which is recycled 30 gallons of oil are saved, so it is well worth making the effort.

Paper

Left in a landfill, a single bus ticket takes a year to degrade. The paper used for UK newspapers in just one year would wrap around the Earth 270 times. Paper can be recycled up to seven times, although we only recycle about 25 per cent of the paper we use in the UK, compared with around 60 per cent in some European countries. Every tonne of paper recycled saves 17 trees and 7,000 gallons of water. Recycling paper also uses less electricity and creates fewer emissions than making new paper.

Products that can be made from recycled paper include pens, stationery, folding seats, towels, animal bedding, bags, calendars, photo frames and even coffins.

Aluminium cans and foil

Aluminium cans in landfill sites take around 50 years to degrade – and three billion of them were disposed of this way in 2000. Aluminium can be recycled indefinitely. Recycling aluminium uses 95 per cent less energy than making new aluminium. Aluminium has the highest value of any recyclable packaging material, so it is popular with fund-raisers who can swap large quantities of cans for cash.

Steel cans

More than 400,000 tonnes of steel cans are put into landfills in the UK each year. They take at least 50 years to degrade. Steel is the world's most recycled metal – steel cans are one of the easiest things to separate out for recycling, because they are magnetic. Recycling steel saves resources such as iron ore, coal and water. It also reduces emissions and energy used in the extraction, transportation and transformation of these materials.

Products that can be made from recycled steel include scissors, furniture, cutlery, jewellery, paperclips and other cans.

Plastic bottles

A plastic bottle will take around 450 years to degrade in a landfill. Plastics are made from oil – a valuable non-renewable resource. The six most common types of plastic can all be easily recycled. Recycled plastic can be used for many things – compost bins, recycling containers, furniture, pens, bags – even fleeces.

Batteries

Many batteries contain toxic heavy metals, which can be harmful to the environment and human health. Check the labels and make sure that you choose ones which are cadmium free. Many local authorities will collect unwanted car batteries, but they may not take batteries used for radios, television remote controls, toys and torches, so speak to your local authority recycling officer. Another option is to use rechargeable batteries or an alternative technology, such as a clockwork mechanism or solar power. However, rechargeable batteries still contain cadmium and should be disposed of as hazardous household waste. Contact the Centre for Alternative Technology (CAT)* or Green Choices* for more information on cadmium-free batteries or alternatives to batteries.

Furniture

Many charities will take unwanted furniture, as long as it is in good condition. Some high street charity shops may also take small items of furniture, but you must make sure that all soft furnishings meet 1988 Fire Safety Regulations (so they must have correct labels still attached). Alternatively, contact the Furniture Recycling Network*. For larger items get in touch with your local authority or second-hand shops to organise a collection.

Clothes and textiles

Wool, cotton and acrylic can all be re-spun to make new textiles. Other textiles can be recycled to make roofing felt, cloths and upholstery stuffing. Take old clothes to your local charity shop; alternatively, many supermarkets have clothing banks in their car parks and charities often collect old clothes.

Organic waste

Fruit and vegetable scraps can be made into compost instead of going into the kitchen bin with the packaging and plastic. Some councils encourage this by offering cheap or free compost bins. See Chapter 6 for more about composting.

Electrical goods and appliances

Every year we throw out 470,000 tonnes of household appliances, much of it packed full of toxic chemicals such as bromine, cadmium, lead and mercury. Passing these products on for re-use is often the most environmentally sound thing to do. So, if you are replacing an appliance, remember that you could buy second-hand or 'reconditioned'.

Your local authority is obliged to take unwanted appliances. However, it is not obliged to pick them up for free, and some councils will charge a small fee.

Some manufacturers will pick up old appliances when they deliver new ones, and dispose of them for you, so this is worth checking when you buy. New European legislation regarding waste electrical and electronic equipment will come into effect from 2004, and it is likely that retailers will then have to implement recycling schemes.

Some areas have projects that take household furniture and basic electrical equipment for reuse in low income households. Contact Waste Watch's★ Wasteline for details of schemes in your area and general advice on waste disposal. See Chapter 4 for more about household appliances and 'brown' goods.

Fridges and freezers

Fridges and freezers are now classed as 'hazardous waste' – which means you are not allowed to dump them and must arrange for proper disposal. An EU regulation that came into force in January 2002 requires that the foaming agent or gas in the insulation must be removed before the appliance is finally disposed of. However, at present there is only one plant in the UK that is capable of doing this. If your retailer will not take the old appliance away for you, you must ask your local authority to do so. It may charge a fee of around £30. For further advice, contact Wasteline.

Computers

Computers are one of the most toxic sources of household waste. There is currently no nationally co-ordinated recycling scheme, although your local authority may be able to help. If it cannot, try contacting Computers for Charity★ or, if you live near London, ComputerAid★ (these organisations will accept IBM-compatible PCs of at least Pentium P200 class, but not Apple Macs).

Recycling symbols and claims

Manufacturers use a variety of symbols on their packaging to indicate recycling. Most are variations of the Mobius loop – a triangle made of three arrows. Confusingly, this symbol can mean either that a product is made of recycled material or that the product can be recycled. Often these symbols are accompanied by statements such as '100 per cent recycled' or 'environmentally friendly'.

For a product to be called 'recycled', there is no minimum percentage of it that has to meet this criterion. The government's 'Green Claims Code', which gives guidelines on the information the public can expect to be given about the environmental impact of consumer goods, recommends the percentage content should be stated, along with the sources of waste the material comes from.

Watch out for vague or meaningless phrases such as 'made with concern for the environment', 'environmentally friendly', 'kind to nature' and 'non-polluting'. And symbols with globes, trees and flowers mean nothing, unless they come with a clear explanation about what is being done to help the environment.

You might come across the following descriptions:

- **Recyclable** Many products made from glass, metal, paper or plastic can be recycled. You can take them to your local authority's recycling centres, where there may be suitable bins. Check first with your local authority recycling officer. Alternatively use the recycling banks provided at your local supermarket when you do your weekly or monthly shop.
- **Recycled content** Products sometimes say 'recycled' even when the amount of recycled content is quite low. Helpful labelling will make clear whether this claim applies to the product or packaging, and will state what percentage is recycled.
- **Biodegradable** If a product is biodegradable, it will break down naturally in soil or in water. Most everyday products biodegrade eventually, but some take many years to break down, or they release harmful substances in the process.

Reducing household waste

An effective way of reducing the problem of waste disposal is to reduce the amount of waste you create in the first place. There are several simple ways to cut down household waste:

- only buy products you really need and which have the least possible packaging
- choose products that come in re-usable packaging (milk bottles can be re-used up to 100 times) or in packaging such as glass and paper which you know can be recycled using facilities near you
- buy products such as laundry detergents and cosmetics that come in refillable containers
- buy fruit and vegetables loose rather than pre-packaged
- return all re-usable bottles, such as milk bottles
- buy in bulk to reduce the amount of packaging used.

The cost of recycled products is coming down as demand for them increases, so if you buy them, you will be helping to encourage manufacturers to reduce their prices even more. There is a wide range to choose from including toilet rolls, stationery and even clothes.

Stopping junk mail

Each year we use enough paper to cut down a forest the size of Wales. If you would like to stop junk mail – and the acres of paper it uses – coming through your letterbox, contact the Mailing Preference Service (MPS)★. This is a non-profit making organisation funded by the direct mail industry that enables consumers to have their names and home addresses removed from, or added to, lists used by the industry.

To stop unaddressed mail, try putting a 'No unrequested mail' sign on your letterbox.

Re-using household items

Another great way to reduce waste is to re-use items wherever possible. For example, if more people re-used their old supermarket carrier bags rather than having new ones every time they did their shopping, the savings in oil used to manufacture them would be enormous. Some supermarkets sell their own versions of re-usable carrier bags, which are more durable than the sort normally dispensed at the till.

Global Action Plan★ advises looking for products that come in re-usable packaging – and for which you can buy refills – or that are re-usable themselves. This includes items such as handkerchiefs and non-disposable razors.

Disposal of sanitary products

According to the Women's Environmental Network (WEN)*, the average woman in the developed world uses about 10,000 sanitary product (sanpro) items during her lifetime. It has also been estimated that 2.5 million tampons, 1.4 million sanitary towels and 0.7 million panty liners are flushed down the toilet every day. Not only do the plastic components of these products litter our beaches, posing a threat to human health and damaging coastal and aquatic wildlife, they also cause blockages in waste water systems.

Flushing these items down the toilet increases the need for sewer maintenance and this adds to the pressure on treatment works. As it is estimated that 75 per cent of blocked drains are caused by sanpro items, it is very important to avoid flushing them and to put them in the waste bin instead. From 1995 the 'Bag It and Bin It' campaign – promoted by many environmental groups, water companies and retailers – has actively campaigned on this issue. Other products also covered by the campaign include condoms, bandages and cotton buds – all of which cause problems in sewage treatment works.

WEN supplies a list of manufacturers of alternative products and factsheets on sanpro and menstruation.

Useful websites

www.defra.gov.uk/environment/consumerprod/gcc The government's 'Green Claims Code'

www.doingyourbit.org.uk Government tips for recycling and improving the environment

www.recycledproducts.org.uk Information on where to buy recycled products, maintained by Waste Watch

www.wastepoint.co.uk A database of every recycling facility in the UK

www.wastewatch.org.uk National organisation promoting and encouraging action on waste reduction, re-use and recycling

Chapter 8

Making a difference

Faced with the sheer scale of environmental problems such as global warming, it is no wonder that many people feel they can do little to make a real impact. But our actions can and do make a difference. We may not have direct power to stop the spread of deforestation, but we *can* decide not to buy products from companies we know have a bad environmental record. We can change our current energy supplier. And we can reduce our own 'ecological footprint' by changing to low-energy light bulbs, turning down the thermostat and limiting our use of energy-guzzling appliances.

Most of the small, inexpensive things you can do to be more energy efficient have already been covered elsewhere in this book. In this chapter, we look at some of the more radical ways in which homes can be made to have less impact on the environment. These changes often go hand in hand with living a 'greener' lifestyle. The chapter concludes with examples of buildings in which these design features have been put into practice.

Building for environmental sustainability

Vast amounts of energy are consumed in the production, transportation and maintenance of buildings and building materials. Selecting materials and products which use the least energy can help to cut down the impact this energy consumption has on the environment. This means choosing natural or near-natural materials or products that can be re-used and recycled or that are made from recycled materials (see 'Materials', overleaf).

Making sure that buildings are well insulated will also help to reduce fuel bills and save energy once the house is occupied (see Chapter 3). The design can also incorporate means of harnessing solar energy to provide space heating or hot water (see opposite for more on solar power).

For more information contact the Association for Environment Conscious Building (AECB)*, which promotes the principles of environmental building.

Glazing

Glass can transmit the sun's 'free heat' into buildings and, when used with appropriate design, can make a positive contribution to the home environment. Light wall colourings, strategically positioned mirrors and high-performance glazing all help to make the most of this free energy source. It is important to remember that new glazing should have optimum thermal performance under the new Building Regulations Part L1. Conservatories are the best ordinary example of passive solar heating.

Water and waste

Toilets which use less water are available from specialist suppliers. These systems help to reduce household water consumption (see Chapter 5). A more radical approach is a reed-bed sewage system, which disposes of sewage in an ecologically sound way. But the ultimate 'green loo' is the composting toilet. Composting toilets use no water and, instead, evaporate urine and turn sewage into nutrients, which can be used in the garden. There are also separating toilets, which separate urine from solid waste. The urine can then be piped on to hay or straw bales to produce nitrogen-rich compost.

An additional measure is rainwater harvesting systems (grey-water systems), available from DIY shops or specialist building centres, which save and store rainwater from roofs for re-use in the garden (see Chapter 6).

Materials

A great deal of materials used in building are from finite sources, therefore it is important to use sustainable alternatives. Timber and bio-crops, such as straw – provided they are grown and harvested in a sustainable way – are generally considered to be the most renewable resource. Timber can also be recycled and re-used. Look for timber and wood products with the Forest Stewardships Council (FSC)* logo.

Naturally durable timbers, such as oak, sweet chestnut, larch and red cedar, are expensive and sometimes difficult to source. To provide cheaper alternatives, manufacturers often pre-treat non-durable timbers and sapwoods with fungicidal and insecticidal chemicals. If you use pre-treated timber of this sort, then inorganic borates offer significant health and environmental advantages over fungicidal and insecticidal chemicals. Inorganic borates are simple compounds that have no potential for 'off-gassing'. On disposal, they are easily assimilated into the environment.

Some insulation materials use hydrochlorofluorocarbons (HCFCs), which contribute to ozone depletion as well as global warming. Less harmful alternatives such as cellulose, cork and foamed glass are available.

'Green' products are now stocked in most good DIY shops or specialist building centres, and you can choose from a range of materials such as solar panels, natural paints, clay flooring, etc.

Using alternative technologies in the home

Energy use in buildings accounts for nearly a quarter of the UK's carbon dioxide emissions. Two ways to reduce these are increasing energy efficiency and expanding the role of renewable power sources in electricity generation.

Solar power

At first sight, the huge amounts of 'free' energy available from the sun would appear the most promising option for reducing greenhouse gas emissions. Unfortunately, it is difficult to harness economically. Chapter 2 gives details of large-scale solar energy projects; here, we look at ways solar power can be used in the home.

There are three main ways to use solar energy, each involving its own technology.

- **Passive solar heating**   Space heating by means of designing buildings to make best use of the sun.
- **Solar water heating**   Using solar energy directly to heat water for use in the home.
- **Photovoltaics**   Generating electricity from sunlight.

Passive solar heating

When solar radiation passes through glass, its wavelength is changed and not all of it can escape. This means the radiation is 'trapped', leading to an increase in air temperature in enclosed spaces behind the glass – a phenomenon used in greenhouses and so known as the 'greenhouse effect'. When used in house design, it is known as passive solar heating.

According to NEF Renewables* – part of the National Energy Foundation – passive solar design can provide up to 70 per cent of a building's energy needs. In particular, large glass windows or conservatories (especially those on south-facing surfaces) can take advantage of large amounts of free energy from the sun.

About 14 per cent of space heating in an ordinary British home comes from solar energy passing through walls and windows. What passive solar design aims to do is maximise this energy. This can be best applied in new buildings, where the orientation of the building, the density of surrounding houses, the size and position of the glazed areas, and the composition of other materials used in the structures, are designed to make the most of solar gain. By incorporating passive solar design into new buildings, annual fuel bills can be cut by about a third.

Designing a property to maximise free solar gain need not add to the price of construction. Studies on houses in Milton Keynes have shown that low-cost, passive solar design features, draught-proofing and insulating reduced heating bills by 40 per cent – a saving which paid back the costs of installing these measures within two years.

Solar water heating

Solar water-heating systems are the most popular way in which solar energy is used in the UK. Collectors are normally installed on a roof, which is south-facing, although if this is not possible, then west to south-west, or east to south-east will suffice. Alternatively, collectors can be placed on the ground (these are ideal for use with swimming pools – see opposite). Panels should be angled to the horizontal between 10° and 60°, with 35° being the ideal. Pipes from the system are then connected to the hot-water system.

A solar water-heating system works by pre-heating cold water. This is done in a second hot-water cylinder (the 'solar' or pre-heat cylinder). Here the solar-heated water – separated from the cold water, which enters the cylinder at the bottom – passes through a heating coil, and leaves at the top to go to the main hot-water cylinder. As well as a pump to drive the solar-heated water round its own circuit, various controls are needed to ensure that water flows only when the solar collector is warmer than the pre-heat cylinder, and precautions are necessary to present the system freezing in winter.

It is difficult to use solar water heating where hot water in the home comes from a combination boiler, which heats the water directly without the need for a hot-water cylinder. As a combination boiler is designed to operate on cold water at mains pressure, you need to check with the boiler manufacturer that yours can accept pre-heated (i.e. warm) water at low pressure.

Typical installation costs vary from about £500 for the cheapest DIY system, to £5,500 for the most expensive, professionally installed system. A solar water-heating system can provide approximately 60 per cent of typical domestic hot-water needs in the UK. Only DIY systems (see overleaf), therefore, are likely to pay for themselves in fuel savings.

Using solar energy in a solar water-heating system has very little environmental impact – the main one is generally due to the use of fossil fuels in the manufacture of the solar panels. A correctly installed solar hot-water system should give 20 to 30 years of hot water, cutting bills and greenhouse gas emissions. There are two types of solar water collection: flat plate and evacuated tubes.

Swimming pools

Solar water heating is an ideal application for swimming pools, as the pool water can be circulated directly through the solar collectors and a pumped circuit already exists to take water to a water filter. The collectors can be mounted on the ground (at an angle); alternatively, special swimming pool surrounds are available which incorporate solar collectors that you can walk on.

Flat-plate collectors
A simple flat plate is the most common type of collector. It consists of a specially coated black metal surface, embedded in an insulated

box and covered with glass or clear plastic on the front. Water is fed through the collector in pipes attached to a metal sheet and picks up the heat in the metal. In the UK climate, the water circulating in the pipework must contain non-toxic anti-freeze to protect it from freezing in the winter. The pipes are often made of copper for better conduction.

Flat-plate collectors typically supply pre-heated water at around 35°C (so some additional heating will normally be necessary). They can, however, reach temperatures of 80°C on a very hot day. To have flat-plate collectors professionally installed costs between £2,000 and £4,000.

Evacuated tubes

Evacuated tubes, fitted into insulated steel castings, work by using a vacuum around the collector. The tubes reduce the amount of heat lost from the collector and are suited to colder, cloudier climates, such as that of the UK. They are efficient enough to heat water to temperatures of around 60°C, so the water may not need further heating. They are more expensive than flat-plate collectors. A typical domestic system costs £3,500 to £5,500 if professionally installed.

DIY solar water-heating systems

Solar water heating is a fairly straightforward technology and, as such, the skills required to build and install a typical system are not beyond the expertise of someone who is competent at DIY.

Most solar heating components are readily available from specialist suppliers (sometimes as part of a kit), or from various on-line or 'green' building catalogues. Many of the ancillary components (pumps, pipes and cylinders) are standard plumbing accessories, available from plumbers' and builders' merchants and DIY stores.

Self-build collectors

You can make your own solar collector using central heating radiators (painted black) or 'clip fins' attached to copper pipes. The Centre for Alternative Technology (CAT)* publishes a book called *Solar Water Heating: A DIY Guide*, which tells you how to do this. Its book *Tapping the Sun* explains how to join this collector to your hot-water system, and run a solar water-heating systems course.

The cost of installing a DIY collector is likely to be around £500 for a system measuring four metres square. If radiators can be obtained cheaply or free of charge, installing a collector based on black radiator panels could cost as little as £300.

Installation and suppliers

Fitting solar water-heating panels to most existing buildings does not usually require planning permission, with some exceptions in conservation areas or on listed buildings, but it pays to check. Always seek professional help if you are not sure about installation procedures. You should certainly check that any installation meets the requirements of the Building Regulations and the Water Regulations. If you want a tailor-made system then it is worth finding a parts supplier who is willing to design the plumbing and layout of the system for you, as there are a number of ways to install a system, depending on your budget and space available.

An important consideration is the type of water heating system you have (see Chapter 3 for more about the different systems). Solar heating systems work best with a system using stored hot water in a hot-water cylinder. As mentioned earlier, if you have a combination boiler you need to check if it can accept pre-heated water.

If you are not confident about fitting your own solar water-heating system, you may wish to join a 'Solar Club' (for details contact the Centre for Sustainable Energy★). They provide information, advice and technical support and encourage self-build ventures.

Photovoltaic cells

Photovoltaics (PV) – the direct conversion of solar energy to electricity in a cell – was developed as part of the US space programme. Each cell contains two or more thin layers of semi-conducting material, such as silicon. When exposed to light, electrical charges are generated which are conducted away as direct current.

Photovoltaic electricity is currently almost five times more expensive than conventional electricity and it is reckoned that providing a photovoltaic power supply capable of meeting the demand from a typical domestic energy-efficient house would cost in the region of £20,000.

In remote areas where grid connection is expensive, however, PVs can be the most cost-effective power source. The UK is an exporter of PV technology to countries where grid electricity is expensive or remote.

In the UK, there are at present only six photovoltaic roofs, in contrast to countries such as Germany where there are over 1,000 already in operation, with plans for many more. In March 2002, the Trade and Industry Secretary announced a £20 million solar-power funding programme, which could increase the number of domestic PV installations in the UK tenfold by 2005. In addition, the European Commission has set a target of one million roofs clad with PV by the year 2010. As the scale of production increases, prices will fall and PV will ultimately become commonplace.

The Energy Saving Trust (EST)★ can provide a 50 per cent grant for PV installations for domestic customers and grants for larger-scale projects as well. (see Appendix II at the back of this book for more details).

Building Regulations approval may be required for photovoltaic panels, as extra rafters may have to be put in to support the heavy panels, but this is usually easy to obtain. Additional wiring will certainly be required and you may also need to replace electricity meters to measure the electricity flowing to and from the National Grid if you 'sell' excess electricity.

At the present state of development, you are far more likely to encounter photovoltaics in small-scale use for things such as security lights, pond pumps, battery chargers, solar-powered radios and calculators.

Wind power

The use of wind energy in the UK ranges from large wind farms producing electricity competitive with conventional power stations (see Chapter 2) to small battery-charging applications. The British Wind Energy Association★ can provide a list of UK manufacturers and distributes factsheets on small wind turbine systems.

Alternative technology design and build companies

A few specialist companies design and supply small- to medium-sized customised solar and wind systems including portable solar power units. These units, which can power lights, laptop computers, answering machines, TVs, small power tools and medical equipment, are suitable for remote dwellings or for use as a power back-up system where the grid is unreliable.

Alternative technology in operation

The Centre for Alternative Technology (CAT)* located in Machynlleth in Wales has been putting the principles of sustainable living into practice for over 20 years. It has become a showcase for new and renewable technology including wind, solar and hydro power. You can visit for the day or stay for a residential course on everything from wind energy to composting toilets and straw-bale house building. CAT also produces a large range of books on renewable energy and has an on-line shop.

Examples of 'green' homes in the UK

Although most householders will concentrate on energy-saving measures they can adopt in existing buildings, some pioneering projects show how recent advances can be utilised in custom-built, low-energy homes. For more examples of such projects, contact Sustainable Homes★.

The Gaia Centre

The Gaia Energy Centre★ at Delabole in Cornwall demonstrates the benefits of using alternative sources of power. The building itself is very much part of the exhibition. Electrical energy is supplied from a wind turbine, while energy features such as solar roofing panels, computer-controlled heating, ventilation systems and a greywater system make the Gaia Centre about 50 per cent more energy efficient than a normal building of similar size.

Materials used in the Centre's construction come from sustainable sources and were carefully chosen for their ability to blend in with the surrounding landscape.

155

Self-build projects

While many first-time buyers continue to struggle to get on the property ladder, some are grouping together to build their own homes. More than 100 groups in the UK are now living in self-built communities.

One such group is the Hedgehog Self-Build Co-op* in Brighton – sponsored by Brighton Council and the South London Family Housing Association. The Hedgehog community consists of ten timber-framed, terraced, energy-efficient houses made from renewable materials. Each member has the right to rent a house from the Group's association in perpetuity and can then pass it on to future generations. The rent is around 75 per cent of the market level, as a lifelong reward for members' construction work.

The Round House

In 1986 the Round House in Milton Keynes was one of 50 show houses built for the Energy World exhibition and provided a testing ground for what later became the National Home Energy Rating Scheme (NHER) – see Chapter 1.

The Round House – famous for being buried beneath the ground in a thick insulating blanket of soil – boasts a conical roof intended to minimise external surfaces and cold areas, thus reducing heat loss. Features include passive solar gain, underfloor heating, a ducted heat exchange system and a mechanical ventilation system.

The National Energy Centre

The National Energy Centre* in Milton Keynes serves as a focal point for the sustainable use of energy not only in Milton Keynes but throughout the UK. It demonstrates that high energy-efficiency can be an integral part of building design without adding additional costs to the overall build and design process. This is exemplified by a careful combination of site orientation, window design, high insulation levels and high thermal mass.

Additional features include a small photovoltaic array and a wind-powered light which illuminates the main entrance.

'E-Houses' at Kings Hill

In February 2002 work began on a number of 'E-Houses' at the Kings Hill Development★ in West Malling, Kent. Features include specially designed prefabricated walls, which keep heat in and damp out, while allowing moisture to escape. A heating and monitoring system regulates air flow and ventilation throughout the building, halving heat loss and using around 30 per cent less energy than in a conventional home.

The INTEGER House

The INTEGER★ Millennium House, built in Watford, demonstrates and evaluates the use of sustainable materials and 'green' energy sources. The house was designed, built and occupied within eighteen weeks and suppliers donated materials, expertise and time free of charge. Materials were selected for sustainability, low embodied energy, long life and low maintenance, and the whole process was featured in the BBC's DreamHouse programme. In the four years since it opened, over 5,000 people have visited the house.

The Nottingham Ecohome

Unlike the other projects featured in this chapter, the Nottingham Ecohome★ demonstrates energy-saving modifications that can be made to an existing house.

This three-storey, five-bedroom Victorian property in West Bridgford, Nottingham, belongs to Penney Poyzer and her husband Gil. The house is being renovated ecologically and used as a laboratory to test new products from the eco-building market.

Key features of the house are: energy conservation through high levels of insulation; water conservation through rainwater collection; reduction of sewage output by use of a composting system; reduction of waste; and the use of non-toxic finishes. The roof insulation, heat-recovery fans and high-performance glazing also work to reduce heat loads, while a solar collector contributes towards the water heating.

The exterior of the solid brick walls has 150mm insulation, and the underside of the timber floors above the cellar is insulated with 160mm natural material.

The Nottingham
Ecohome

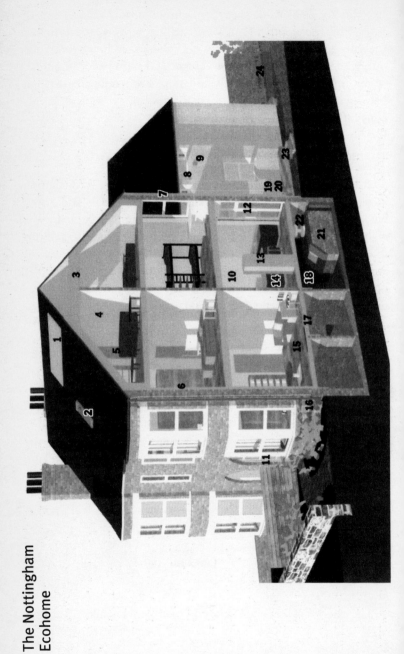

Features at a glance

1 Flat-plate solar collectors for heating water

2 Roof insulation 300/400mm thick, made of shredded surplus newspapers

3 Roof lights with insulating (low emissivity) glass

4 Natural plasters – clay and lime based

5 Super-insulated hot-water tank

6 100mm ozone-friendly drylining to front face to maintain exterior brick appearance

7 150mm expanded polystyrene (EPS) exterior wall insulation with rendered finish

8 Space-saving bath and thermostatic shower controls can save water

9 Heat-recovery fans limit ventilation heat loss

10 Environmentally friendly paints

11 Draught lobby in porch

12 Triple- and double-glazed timber windows treated with natural fungicides and stains

13 Energy-efficient appliances

14 Second-hand, natural and reclaimed furniture

15 Stripped floorboards

16 Copper rainwater goods with filter for rain harvesting

17 160mm hemp/woodwool (incorporating air-tightness improvements) floor insulation

18 Rainwater storage for use in WCs, washing machine and outside tap

19 Low-flush WCs

20 Non-PVC waste pipes

21 Composting chamber for solid waste from WCs

22 Separator lets liquids drain off and solids into composting chamber

23 Decking from English green oak provides longevity without toxic pressure treatment

24 Organic land management utilising the principles of permaculture

BedZED

Housing associations and local authorities are actively encouraging a greener government agenda in eco-housing through initiatives such as Best Value and Local Agenda 21. The most advanced of these innovative schemes is the Beddington Zero Energy Development (BedZED) in Sutton, which is being built by the Peabody Housing Trust* and comprises 82 energy-efficient, sustainable homes. Everything about the scheme, from the layout and the building materials to the heating supply, has been designed to cut energy consumption.

BedZED uses energy only from renewable sources generated on site and is the first large-scale 'carbon neutral' community – in other words, it does not to add to the amount of carbon dioxide in the atmosphere. It is also a 'zero energy' development – it will not use more energy than it produces.

The buildings have been designed to conserve energy in the following ways.

- Super-insulated roofs, walls and floors drastically reduce heat loss by allowing heat from the sun, lights, appliances, hot water and everyday activities such as cooking to keep the houses warm.
- Triple-glazed windows and timber frames, coupled with well-sealed windows and doors further reduce heat loss. A heat exchanger in the wind-driven ventilation system recovers between 50 and 70 per cent of the warmth from the outgoing stale air.
- All homes are fitted with photovoltaic solar panels, making the most of their south-facing position and allowing for conversion of the sun's energy into electricity. This will be used to power recharging points for electric vehicles.
- Kitchens are fitted with the latest in energy-saving appliances and low-energy lighting.

It is estimated that compared to a typical suburban home, residents might see a 60 per cent reduction in total energy demand and a 90 per cent reduction in heat demand.

Further reading

Chiras, D.D. *The Natural House: A Complete Guide to Healthy, Energy-efficient, Environmental Homes.* Chelsea Green, 2000

Gipe, P. *Wind Energy Basics: A Guide to Small and Micro Wind Systems.* Chelsea Green, 1999

Harland, E. *Eco-Renovation – The ecological home improvement guide.* Green Books Ltd, 1993

Horne, B. and Geddes, P. *Tapping the Sun: A Guide to Solar Water Heating.* Centre for Alternative Technology, 2000

Kachadorian, J. *The Passive Solar House: Using Solar Design to Heat and Cool Your Home.* Chelsea Green, 1997

Ramsey, D. *Complete Idiots Guide to Solar Power for Your Home.* Alpha Books, 2002

Roaf, S. *Ecohouse: a Design Guide.* Architectural Press, 2001

Strong et al. *The Solar Electric House: Energy for the Environmentally-responsive, Energy-independent Home.* Chelsea Green, 1995

Trimby, P. *Solar Water Heating: A DIY Guide.* Centre for Alternative Technology, 2000

Appendix I

'Green' electricity suppliers

The following list details some of the suppliers that offer 'green' electricity (and one that supplies green gas) in the UK. For more advice on choosing the right deal for your requirements, and for information about prices in your area, visit www.greenprices.co.uk. Remember that you may pay more for green electricity than for electricity from non-renewable sources, although prices can vary from region to region. Be aware also that some suppliers quote prices inclusive of VAT, which may make them appear more expensive than those that do not. Check with the supplier before making your final choice.

AMERADA GAS: Climate Care Tariff
Customer Services
Selectapost 620
Claypit Lane
Leeds
L52 AQJ
Tel: (0845) 305 3000
Website: www.amerada.co.uk

How it works Unlike other green tariffs, this one is for gas. It funds the work of Climate Care, an organisation that works to offset the effects of carbon dioxide produced by burning gas and other fossil fuels. This is done both by investing money in renewable energy and energy efficiency programmes, and by replanting deforested and degraded sites around the world to 'soak up' the carbon dioxide.

How much it costs A proportion of the money you pay for your gas (0.119p per kWh) goes to Climate Care. Amerada also makes an additional £10 payment for every customer who signs up to the tariff.

ECOTRICITY: Ecotricity
Axiom House
Station Road
Stroud
Gloucestershire
GL5 3AP
Tel: (01453) 756111
Website: www.ecotricity.co.uk

How it works Ecotricity's domestic supply is due to be launched in April 2003. It is available throughout England and Wales and is the same price as conventional electricity from the main local supplier in each region. Each year, Ecotricity will replace a minimum of 10 per cent of the electricity its customers use with new green electricity. This is incremental (i.e. in the second year at least 20 per cent will be generated from green sources).

How much it costs At the time of writing no prices were available.

Renewable energies Wind.

GREEN ENERGY (UK) PLC: Green Energy 100% and Green Energy 10%
9 Church Street
Ware
Hertfordshire
SG12 9EG
Tel: (01920) 486156
Website: www.greenenergy.uk.com

How it works Customers can choose between two tariffs – Green Energy 100% or Green Energy 10%. With the latter 10 per cent of your electricity will come from renewable sources. Green Energy 100% is 'pure green' electricity. The company allocates 50 per cent of its profits to renewable generation projects.

How much it costs Prices vary from region to region, but are inclusive of VAT. Green Energy 10% prices are set at the same level as your regional electricity company; Green Energy 100% costs a premium of 8 per cent on a standard tariff. Customers receive free shares in the company. Payment is by direct debit only.

Renewable energies Mainly in the UK, these include wind, hydro-electric, solar, tidal, and renewable energy from small-scale producers.

LONDON ELECTRICITY: Green Tariff

Templar House
81–87 High Holborn
London
WC1V 6NU
Tel: 020-7242 9050
Website: www.london-electricity.co.uk

How it works When customers sign up to the Green Tariff they will be contributing to the Green Energy Fund. This fund is used for renewable energy projects such as solar panels for a school or wind power for a hospice.

How much it costs For the average customer, the Green Tariff will cost an additional £13.20 per year. This amount is matched by London Electricity and paid into the Green Energy Fund. Customers also receive an energy-efficiency pack which includes two energy-efficient light bulbs.

Renewable energies Wind, landfill gas and small-scale hydro-electric.

NORTHERN IRELAND ELECTRIC (NIE): Eco Energy (domestic)

120 Malone Road
Belfast
NI 26041
Tel: (08457) 455455
Website: www.nie.co.uk

How it works Some, or all, of your electricity will be supplied from renewable sources, and NIE will match each unit you use with energy from renewable sources. The first round of the Eco Energy Fund made grants to 12 renewable energy projects.

Renewable energies Solar, wind, hydro-electric.

NPOWER: Juice
Oak House
Bridgwater Road
Warndon
Worcester
WR4 9FP
Tel: (0800) 316 2610
Email: juice@npower.com
Website: www.npower.com

How it works Juice is provided by npower in partnership with Greenpeace. At the time of writing Juice electricity comes from onshore wind and hydro-electric, but from autumn 2003 Juice will be provided entirely from the new North Hoyle Offshore Wind Farm, when its construction and commissioning is complete.

How much it costs If you are already with npower you can switch to Juice for no extra cost. If you apply for Juice electricity on its own and pay by direct debit, you will get a 3 per cent discount from your bill. If you choose both Juice and gas, and pay both by direct debit, the discount will increase to 7 per cent. Contact npower for details of tariffs if you are not an existing customer.

Renewable energies Wind, hydro-electric.

POWERGEN: GreenPlan
Phoenix Centre
Colliers Way
Nottingham
NG8 6AL
Tel: (0800) 363363
Website: www.powergen.co.uk/greenplan

How it works The GreenPlan tariff includes an automatic donation to a green fund for every unit of electricity you use. The fund is used to support new energy generation projects with a strong community theme, such as solar panels for churches, ground sourced heat pumps for homes, etc.

How much it costs For an average customer the GreenPlan donation will cost £9 per year. Powergen will match this donation, taking the total to £18 per year. There is a GreenPlan option for standard and Economy 7 electricity, and for all payment methods including pre-payment.

Renewable energies Wind, hydro-electric.

SCOTTISH HYDRO-ELECTRIC: RSPB Energy
200 Dunkeld Road
Perth
PH1 3GH
Tel: (0845) 300 2141
Website: www.hydro.co.uk

See Scottish and Southern Energy plc

SCOTTISHPOWER: Green Energy
Cathcart Business Park
Spean Street
Glasgow
G44 4BE
Tel: (0800) 027 7774
Email: customer.services@scottishpower.co.uk
Website: www.scottishpower.co.uk

How it works The Green Energy Fund helps fund new renewable energy projects. It is administered by The Green Energy Trust, which comprises renewable energy experts, environmental organisations and representatives from the ScottishPower Group. Projects supported by the fund include small-scale wind and solar energy schemes in community and educational settings.

How much it costs A fixed daily contribution of 2.74p is added to the standard ScottishPower electricity prices for your area and donated on your behalf to the Green Energy Fund. This donation is matched by ScottishPower.

Renewable energies Wind, hydro-electric.

SCOTTISH AND SOUTHERN ENERGY (SSE) PLC: RSPB Energy

Grampian House
200 Dunkeld Road
Perth
PH1 3GH
Tel: (0800) 117116
Website: www.scottishandsouthern.co.uk

Regional subsidiaries: Southern Electric, Scottish Hydro-Electric *and* SWALEC

How it works For every household signing up to RSPB Energy, £20 (£10 for electricity, £10 for gas) is donated to the Royal Society for the Protection of Birds (RSPB). An additional £10 (£5 for electricity and £5 for gas) is contributed each year you remain with the scheme. The RSPB uses the money to buy and manage land for nature reserves and Scottish and Southern Energy buys green electricity to match your usage.

How much it costs The tariff costs no more than electricity from your local supplier.

Renewable energies Hydro-electric, landfill gas and wind.

SEEBOARDENERGY LTD: Go Green Fund & Greenlight (domestic lighting)

Supply Business
PO Box 639
329 Portland Road
Hove
East Sussex
BN3 5SY
Tel: (0800) 581255
Website: www.seeboardenergy.com

How it works You pay extra for the Go Green Fund, which is spent on developing green energy. All customer contributions are matched, up to a combined maximum of £250,000 a year, creating a potential annual fund of £500,000. An independent Green Fund Trust allocates all the money to renewable energy projects.

How much it costs Customers pay an extra 0.5p (ex. VAT) over standard quarterly, standard domestic or Economy 7 electricity tariffs, which works out at about £15 per year for the average customer. Go Green does not apply to your gas bill, even with dual fuel.

Renewable energies Solar, wind, hydro-electric.

SERVISTA: Servista.GreenPower

32–38 Saffron Hill
Farringdon
London
EC1N 8FH
Tel: (0870) 241 2732
Website: www.servista.com

How it works Servista can provide green electricity to all customers in England and Wales who have a credit meter and who wish to pay by direct debit.

How much it costs Servista.GreenPower costs the average customer (who switches from their regional electricity company and consumes the average 3,300 kWh per annum) an extra £1 per month.

Renewable energies Wind, hydro-electric.

SOUTHERN ELECTRIC: RSPB Energy

Grampian House
200 Dunkeld Road
Perth
PH1 3GH
Tel: (08457) 444555
Website: www.southern-electric.co.uk

See Scottish and Southern Energy plc

SOUTH WESTERN ELECTRICITY BOARD (SWEB):
Green Tariff
Sowton Industrial Estate
Osprey Road
Exeter
EX2 7HZ
Tel: (0800) 328 9026
Website: www.sweb.co.uk

How it works Your electricity consumption is matched with energy from renewable sources. The money goes into a fund which is used to invest in community and educational renewable energy projects.

How much it costs You pay an extra 0.4p per unit (£13.20 per year for the average customer) and SWEB matches this contribution. You also receive an energy-efficiency pack, which includes a free home energy survey, information on energy-efficiency grants, energy-efficiency advice and two energy-saving light bulbs.

Renewable energies Wind, hydro-electric.

SWALEC (South Wales Electricity): RSPB Energy
Grampian House
200 Dunkeld Road
Perth
PH1 3GH
Tel: (0800) 052 5252
Website: www.swalec.co.uk

See Scottish and Southern Energy plc

UNIT ENERGY LTD: UNIT[E]
Freepost (SCE9229)
Chippenham
SN15 1UZ
Tel: (0845) 601 1410
Website: www.unit-e.co.uk

How it works Unit[e] supplies only 100 per cent renewable energy. There is an additional cost to customers for this product, which 'is directly related to the cost of supplying an environmental good'.

Unit[e] purchases renewable power from wind farms and small hydro-electric power stations across the UK.

Renewable energies Wind, hydro-electric.

YORKSHIRE ELECTRICITY: Juice

Pyre House
Birchwood Drive
Blackenhill Business Park
Peterlee
SR8 2RS
Tel: (0800) 073 3000
Website: www.yeg.co.uk

See npower

Appendix II

Financial help with energy efficiency

There are a number of government and local authority grants available in England, Wales, Scotland and Northern Ireland to help with energy efficiency improvements in the home. The following table outlines the main ones that are available at the time of writing. Many of these grants are open only to people who are in receipt of benefits or who are aged over 60 (see table for eligibility details). The criteria vary from region to region.

It is worth contacting the Energy Saving Trust (EST)★ for details of the schemes available in your particular region.

Energy suppliers themselves also offer energy-efficiency incentives to householders. Under the government's Energy Efficiency Commitment (EEC), set up by Defra, all major gas and electricity suppliers are obliged to run schemes aimed at improving energy-efficiency in homes. Suppliers will probably need to spend around £500 million by 2005 in order to meet their targets, and at least half of the energy savings should be from the homes of those on low incomes. The schemes are monitored by OFGEM★, which sets the target for each supplier and ensures compliance.

These schemes are not necessarily open only to the suppliers' customers, but to find out more you could start by contacting your own supplier.

There are also a number of community groups that have been set up to insulate homes and fit draught-proofing at low cost for people on low incomes or who are receiving state benefits. For more details contact your local authority.

Provider	Scheme	Details	Value	Eligibility	Contact
EAGA Partnership	Warm Front (England)	Grants for heating and insulation measures in households with the greatest health risks. A Warm Front grant can provide a package drawn from the following. Insulation: • Loft insulation • Draught-proofing • Cavity wall insulation • Hot-water tank insulation. Heating systems: • Gas room heaters with thermostat controls • Electric storage heaters with thermostat controls • Converting a solid-fuel open fire to a glass-fronted fire • Timer controls for electric space and water heaters. Extra measures: • Energy advice • Two low-energy light bulbs • Hot-water tank jacket.	Maximum grant of £1,500.	Householders who have a child under 16 or are pregnant and have been given a MATB1 maternity certificate, and are also in receipt of one or more of the following benefits: • Income Support • Housing Benefit • Council Tax Benefit • Income-based JobSeeker's Allowance • Working Families' Tax Credit. Householders who are receiving one or more of the following benefits: • Income Support (which must include a disability premium) • Housing Benefit (which must include a disability premium) • Council Tax Benefit (which must include a disability premium) • Disabled Person's Tax Credit • Attendance Allowance • Industrial Injuries Disablement Benefit (which must include Constant Attendance Allowance) • War Disablement Pension (which must include the mobility supplement or Constant Attendance Allowance).	Customer Services EAGA Partnership Freepost NEA 12054 Newcastle upon Tyne NE2 1BR Tel: (0800) 316 6011, Minicom (0800) 072 0156 Website: www.eaga.co.uk For all queries concerning an existing application, email enquiry@eaga.co.uk

EAGA Partnership	Warm Front Plus (England)	Packages similar to Warm Front (see above) but, in addition to those measures, Warm Front Plus may also offer gas or electric central heating systems.	Maximum grant of £2,500. If the cost of the work is higher than this the installer will inform you of the extra cost before you agree to the work. If you cannot afford the extra cost the measures will be revised.	Claimants must be aged over 60 and be in receipt of one or more of the following benefits: • Income Support • Housing Benefit • Council Tax Benefit • Income-Based JobSeeker's Allowance.	As Warm Front
EAGA Partnership	Warm Deal (Scotland)	Energy advice and grants for the following energy-efficiency measures: • Cavity wall insulation • Loft insulation • Draught-proofing.	Maximum grant of £500.	Claimants under the age of 60 must be in receipt of one of the following benefits: • Housing Benefit • Family Credit/Working Families' Tax Credit • Attendance Allowance • War Disablement Pension (which must include Constant Attendance Allowance) • Industrial Injuries Disablement Benefit (which must include Constant Attendance Allowance) • Disability Living Allowance • Disability Working Allowance/ Disabled Person's Tax Credit	EAGA Partnership Scotland 74 Commercial Street Commercial Quay Edinburgh EH6 6LX Tel: 0131-777 2501 Email: Scotland.enquiries@ eaga.co.uk Website: www.eaga.co.uk For all queries concerning an existing application, email enquiry@eaga.co.uk

continued overleaf

Provider	Scheme	Details	Value	Eligibility	Contact
EAGA Partnership	Warm Deal (Scotland) *continued*			• Income-Based JobSeekers' Allowance • Council Tax Benefit • Income Support. Claimants aged 60 or over but who are not in receipt of one of the above benefits will receive a restricted grant of £125 or 25% of the cost of the work, whichever is the lower.	
EAGA Partnership	The Central Heating Programme (Scotland)	A package of measures which includes: • A central heating system • Loft, tank and pipe insulation • Cavity wall insulation • Draught-proofing • A carbon monoxide detector (except where the heating system is electric) • A mains-linked smoke detector and a cold alarm • Energy advice • An optional check of entitlement to state benefits.	Based on the recommendations of the programme's surveyor, who will assess the property. Any work in excess of these recommendations will not be covered.	Claimants must be aged 60 or over, resident in Scotland, and be owner-occupiers or private-sector tenants. In addition, claimants must have been resident at the address for a period of 12 months prior to the date of application and intend to stay there for a minimum of 12 months from the date on which the works are completed. This must be their main or only residence. The property must be self-contained and have no central heating, OR the central heating system must be completely broken and beyond repair. Claimants must not have previously claimed a grant at the same address under this scheme.	Eaga Partnership Scotland 74 Commercial Street Commercial Quay Edinburgh EH6 6LX Tel: (0800) 316 1653 Website: www.eaga.co.uk For all queries concerning an existing application, email enquiry@eaga.co.uk

EAGA Partnership	The Home Energy Efficiency Scheme (HEES) (Wales)	A range of energy-efficiency measures for insulation and heating. HEES provides grants for energy-efficiency measures and energy advice.	HEES: maximum grant of £1,500. HEES Plus: maximum grant of £2,700.	The scheme is aimed at owner-occupiers and those who rent their homes from private landlords. It is targeted at people in receipt of certain benefits. HEES is for families with children under 16.	EAGA Partnership Wales Unit 4, Ty Nant Court Ty Nant Road Morganstown Cardiff CF15 8LW Tel: (0800) 316 2815 Email: enquiries.wales@eaga.co.uk Website: www.eaga.co.uk
	HEES Plus (Wales)	HEES Plus offers grants for heating and insulation improvements.		HEES Plus is for lone-parent families with children under 16, people aged 60 or over, and those who are disabled or chronically sick.	For all queries concerning an existing application, email enquiry@eaga.co.uk
EAGA Partnership	The Warm Homes Scheme (Northern Ireland)	A range of energy-efficiency measures for insulation and heating. The Warm Homes Scheme offers grants for insulation and heating improvements.	Warm Homes: maximum grant of £750. Warm Homes Plus: maximum grant of £2,700.	Claimants for the Warm Homes Scheme must be owner-occupiers or private-sector tenants and be in receipt of one of a range of benefits, and have a child under 16.	EAGA Partnership Northern Ireland Dinree House Thomas Street Dungannon County Tyrone BT70 1HN Tel: (028) 8775 3636 Website: www.eaga.co.uk
	The Warm Homes Plus Scheme (Northern Ireland)	The Warm Homes Plus Scheme offers grants for an enhanced package of heating and insulation measures, including central heating.		Claimants for Warm Homes Plus must be aged 60 and over and be owner-occupiers or private-sector tenants.	For all queries concerning an existing application, email enquiry@eaga.co.uk

Provider	Scheme	Details	Value	Eligibility	Contact
A partnership led by the Energy Saving Trust (EST)*	Solar Grants	Grants towards the installation of solar electricity equipment. Three types of grants are available: • domestic householders • social housing groups • commercial organisations.	Up to 50% 'fixed' grant funding for small-scale applications. Applications are accepted and processed on a rolling basis. (Call or check website for information on when the next round of funding becomes available.)	Funding for small-scale applications is available to the following: • Homeowners • SMEs (small/medium enterprises – i.e. organisations with fewer than 250 employees and less than £25 million annual turnover) • Public bodies for use on public buildings (e.g. schools, health centres, etc.) • Voluntary/charitable organisations and community groups.	Energy Saving Trust 21 Dartmouth Street London SW1H 9BP Tel: (0800) 298 3978 Website: www.est.org.uk/solar
Thames Valley Energy Efficiency Advice Centre	The Big Green Boiler Scheme	A national project managed by Thames Valley EEAC. Discounts are available to installers to subsidise the installation of gas condensing boilers. Advice on condensing boilers and on choosing an installer is also available. The boilers offered by the scheme are A-rated for energy efficiency.	Discounts of 30–50% off manufacturer's list price	Available to homeowners and tenants in the social housing sector who have a condensing boiler fitted through the scheme.	Thames Valley EEAC WODC Building Avenue 4 Station Lane Witney OX28 4BN Tel: (0800) 028 2855 Website: www.green-boilers.com

| Department of Trade and Industry. The scheme is managed by the Building Research Establishment (BRE)* | Clear Skies Initiative | Grants for renewable energy measures for homeowners and community groups. The following technologies are supported by the scheme: • Solar water heating • Wind turbines • Hydro-electric turbines • Ground-sourced heat pumps • Automated wood-pellet stoves • Wood-fuelled boilers. Grants are also available for photovoltaics (solar electricity) through the Major Demonstration Programme. | Homeowners: grants of between £500 and £5,000. Community groups: grants of up to £100,000. | Details for eligibility may change from time to time as the scheme develops. To qualify for funding, applicants must be UK residents and own the property for which the grant is being applied. The scheme only applies to properties within England, Wales or Northern Ireland. For Scotland, contact the Scottish Community Renewables Initiative (see below). The system must supply a building (mobile homes, caravans, houseboats, etc. are not eligible) and must be designed, installed and commissioned by an accredited installer. Installers will provide an estimate of the annual energy output of the system. In addition, the system must use components that are listed on the DTI's recognised product list. Grants must be spent within one year of the grant offer being made. A maximum of two grants can be awarded per applicant, provided they are for different technologies (e.g. solar and wind). | Clear Skies Initiative BRE Ltd Bucknalls Lane Garston Watford WD25 9XX Tel: (0870) 243 0930 Website: www.clear-skies.org |

Provider	Scheme	Details	Value	Eligibility	Contact
Department of Trade and Industry, and the Scottish Executive	Scottish Community Renewables Initiative (SCRI)	Financial support for a range of renewable technologies including: • Micro hydro-electric turbines • Micro wind turbines • Solar water and space heating • Ground-sourced heat pumps (powered by renewable electricity) • Automated wood-fuelled heating systems • Solar photovoltaics in dwellings not connected to the electricity grid.	Funding is set at 30% of the installed cost. The maximum grant is £4,000. Any capital cost up to £13,300 will attract funding. The householder can spend more than this and still be eligible, but the extra cost will not be covered. Match funding from other public sources for the same system is not allowed.	SCRI grants are available only to owner-occupiers in Scotland. The renewable energy system must supply a building or a permanently sited mobile home and the system must be designed, installed and commissioned by an approved installer. (SCRI will rely on the accreditation process being developed for the Clear Skies programme). In addition, the system must use components approved by the DTI/Scottish Executive. A maximum of two grants per property is available, provided each covers different technologies. All applicants are offered a DIY Home Energy Check by their local Energy Efficiency Advice Centre as part of the application process.	SCRI Northern & Western Isles EEAC 26 Bridge Street Kirkwall Orkney KW15 1HR Tel: (0800) 138 8858 Email: scri@est.co.uk Website: www.est.org.uk/scri/household/

Appendix III

Living a 'greener' life

Throughout this book we have looked at the various ways in which it is possible to save energy, on an everyday basis, within the home. This is a goal that we may pursue for different reasons: either because we simply want to reduce our household bills, or from a desire to 'do our bit' for the environment – or both. This guide has addressed the practicalities of energy-saving rather than the rationale. However, you may be interested in doing more in terms of adopting a more environmentally friendly lifestyle. And although we have focused on the home, there are other significant ways in which we can make a difference in our daily lives – for example, in the area of transport.

The following case study, project example and quiz offer a brief glance at how we, as individuals and within the community, can make a change to a more 'low-impact' lifestyle. If you would like to find out more you could start with the websites listed later in this appendix. (Some of these organisations are also listed in the 'Useful contacts' section at the back of this book.)

Case study

A couple from Fareham, with four children, expressed a desire to live a more environmentally friendly life. As part of the research for an article in December 2000, *Which?* helped them to achieve these aims in three key areas: energy, transport and waste.

At the start of the 'makeover', the family were concerned that they would not be able to achieve much more than they currently did. They recycled, walked when they could and had two low-energy light bulbs. They also lived in a modern house which had energy-efficient features such as double glazing and loft insulation.

When interviewed, they expressed some concerns that many of us would be familiar with, including time and money: '… driving comes ahead of walking to save time, low-energy light bulbs cost more and using the tumble-drier takes less effort'.

The family filled in a questionnaire from Global Action Plan (GAP)★ about transport, waste, energy and water use, and scored 43 per cent – worse than the national average of 58 per cent. Every month for three months, they received an Action at Home pack from GAP, which cost around £12 and contained practical guidance on living a greener lifestyle.

After three months of using the action packs, the family completed another questionnaire to get their final green score. The changes they had made increased their score to 69 per cent. They made the greatest improvement in energy saving, although they were able to increase their transport score simply by planning their journeys and following other easy tips. They found that they also saved the most money with the energy pack. They managed to implement several changes that cost less than £10 to achieve, but which ultimately resulted in their making savings on their fuel bills.

The family's verdict was that the action packs '. . . jolt you into action – but without making you feel guilty'.

These Action at Home packs have now been superseded by *Ergo*, a quarterly lifestyle and consumer guide to sustainable living from GAP; annual subscription £14.

Eco-teams

The Eco-teams programme is an environmental project that is being piloted in Rushcliffe, Nottingham. It is supported by Global Action Plan (GAP)★ and is being funded by Biffaward, a sustainable waste management scheme, and Rushcliffe Borough Council.

The programme is new to the UK, but in the Netherlands it is a highly successful project that has been taken up by over 10,000 households.

Essentially an Eco-team is a group of six to eight households that participate in eight meetings over a six- to seven-month period, each lasting approximately an hour. A few minutes each week are spent on measuring progress. A team coach or a project co-ordinator is normally available to help with any queries people may have about the programme and can provide practical help with measuring and implementing the scheme.

The Eco-team members are given advice on the following topics: waste, electricity, gas, water, transport and consumer behaviour (such as how and where to shop). As part of the team, participants are helped to become more aware of these issues and to save money and resources.

Through measuring improvements, the aim is that a household will be able to change its way of living, thereby playing its part towards a cleaner, more sustainable future.

For more information about Eco-teams, contact GAP.

Useful websites

www.commonground.org.uk Common Ground (campaigning to preserve local environment and community)

www.cse.org.uk Centre for Sustainable Energy★ (provides energy-efficiency advice, working with local authorities to raise awareness and improve schemes)

www.earthwatch.org Earthwatch (worldwide initiatives to conserve resources)

www.ethical-junction.org Ethical Junction (ethical services, suppliers and virtual 'shopping village')

www.foe.co.uk Friends of the Earth★ (environmental pressure group)

www.futureforests.com Future Forests (tree planting to offset carbon dioxide emissons)

www.globalactionplan.org.uk Global Action Plan★ (working with organisations to help local and environmental problems)

www.greendirectory.net Green Directory★ (listings of green shops, companies and suppliers)

www.greenpeace.org.uk Greenpeace★ (worldwide environmental campaign organisation)

www.groundwork.org.uk Groundwork (local environmental regeneration in UK communities)

www.livingearth.org.uk Living Earth Foundation (community development in the UK and overseas)

www.ukace.org Association for the Conservation of Energy (lobbying group to raise awareness and assess schemes)

Quiz : How green are you?

Energy

What is your average quarterly energy bill?
(include your gas, electricity and/or oil bills over the last year)

Over £250 per month	**1 point** ☐
£200 to £249 per month	**4 points** ☐
£150 to £199 per month	**8 points** ☐
Under £150 per month	**12 points** ☐

Which of the following energy-saving measures do you have in your home?

Gas condensing boiler	**6 points** ☐
Cavity or external wall insulation	**5 points** ☐
Loft insulation of at least 150mm	**5 points** ☐
Draught-proofing around doors and windows	**4 points** ☐
Secondary/double glazing	**3 points** ☐
Hot-water tank insulated/no hot-water storage	**4 points** ☐
Thermostatic radiator valves	**2 points** ☐
Low-energy fridge/freezer	**2 points** ☐
At least one energy-saving light bulb	**1 point** ☐
Shelves above some/all radiators	**1 point** ☐
Foil behind radiators	**1 point** ☐

Do you regularly use any of these methods of saving energy?

Clothes dried naturally (as opposed to the tumble-drier)	**3 points** ☐
Energy-saving cooking techniques (lids on pans, etc.)	**2 points** ☐
Washing machine used on low-temperature settings	**1 point** ☐
TV and video not left on standby	**1 point** ☐
Deduct 4 points if you sometimes leave the heating on when the house is empty	**−4 points** ☐
Deduct 4 points if you burn coal on a real fire	**−4 points** ☐
Deduct 2 points if you have a flame-effect gas fire as well as central heating	**−2 points** ☐
Total score for energy use	☐

Water

Do you cut down on water use by any of the following means?

Take showers rather than baths (excluding power showers)	**4 points** ☐
Flush-reducing device in cistern or low-flush toilet	**2 points** ☐
Taps not left running for teeth cleaning, dishwashing, etc.	**3 points** ☐
Full loads in washing machine	**2 points** ☐
Rainwater butt for garden watering	**2 points** ☐
Car washed with bucket, not hosepipe (or not washed at all)	**1 point** ☐
Garden watered with watering can or other water-saving method, rather than hose or sprinkler	**1 point** ☐
Low-water-use washing machine	**1 point** ☐
Low-water-use dishwasher or no dishwasher	**1 point** ☐
Deduct 2 points if you always have baths rather than a shower	**–2 points** ☐
Deduct 2 points if you water the garden with a sprinkler	**–2 points** ☐
Deduct 2 points if you wash up under running water	**–2 points** ☐
Total score for water conservation	☐

Waste

What is the average amount of rubbish you throw out per week?

More than one rubbish bag per person	**1 point** ☐
One bag per person	**2 points** ☐
Less than one bag per person	**4 points** ☐

What waste do you compost or recycle?

Most kitchen and garden waste composted	**4 points** ☐
All drinks cans recycled	**2 points** ☐
All food/petfood cans recycled	**2 points** ☐
All newspapers and magazines recycled	**2 points** ☐
Oil, paint and solvents disposed of at a recycling centre	**2 points** ☐
Dispose of electrical goods/appliances responsibly	**2 points** ☐
All glass jars and bottles recycled	**1 point** ☐
All plastic bottles recycled	**1 point** ☐

Take clothes for recycling or to a charity shop, etc.	1 point	☐
Pass on unwanted furniture	1 point	☐
Always combine trips to the recycling centre with other journeys	1 point	☐
Deduct 4 points if you don't recycle anything	−4 points	☐
Total score for waste reduction and recycling		☐

Food and shopping

How do you normally do the bulk of your food shopping?

Use local shops within walking/cycling distance	4 points	☐
Travel by public transport to shops	3 points	☐
Drive to supermarket but do at least 1 week's shopping in one go	1 point	☐
Deduct 4 points if you always drive to the shops	−4 points	☐

Which of the following do you do regularly?

Buy some organic vegetables each week	2 points	☐
Grow some of your own vegetables	2 points	☐
Deliberately select products with minimal packaging	2 points	☐
Buy milk or drinks in returnable bottles	2 points	☐
Buy products made from recycled materials (e.g. toilet paper, bin bags)	1 point	☐
Avoid buying strong chemicals if possible	1 point	☐
Take your own shopping bags to the supermarket	1 point	☐
Total score for food and shopping		☐

Transport and travel

How much do you spend on fuel per month?

Over £95 per month	1 point	☐
£70 to £94 per month	2 points	☐
£45 to £69 per month	3 points	☐
Under £45 per month	5 points	☐

Car use – do you:

Own the smallest model for your needs? **2 points** ☐

Use unleaded petrol? **2 points** ☐

Have a catalytic converter? **2 points** ☐

Have your car serviced regularly? **2 points** ☐

Check the tyre pressures regularly? **2 points** ☐

You have a motorcycle or moped instead of a car **15 points** ☐

You don't own a motor vehicle **25 points** ☐

Other journeys – do you:

Choose to walk/cycle instead of using the car 3 times a week? **4 points** ☐

Take public transport instead of the car 3 times a week? **4 points** ☐

Deduct 10 points if you choose to drive to work frequently
even though there is public transport **–10 points** ☐

Deduct 10 points if you have two cars in your household and
you use the second car daily **–10 points** ☐

Deduct 5 points if you have two cars but use the second one
only occasionally **–5 points** ☐

Total score for transport and travel ☐

Results

So, how green are you?

Very green – over 70 points
Good – 55 to 70 points
Fair – 40 to 55 points
Poor – 25 to 40 points
Not at all green – under 25 points

Of course these are not scientific measurements – the issues involved are far too complex – but the ratings provide an indication of everyday environmental impact. The lower you score, the bigger your impact.

You could set yourself a target of improving your score by, say, ten points over one month by implementing some of the energy-saving tips in this book.

Bibliography

Chapter 1 The energy issue

Department of Trade and Industry (DTI). *Energy consumption in the UK.* July 2002

DTI. *Energy – its impact on the environment and society.* July 2002

National Energy Action. *Energy in the Home* (3rd ed). 1996

UK Climate Impacts Programme. *Climate Change Impacts in the UK – The agenda for assessment and action.* 1998

Chapter 2 Energy production and supply

DTI. *Energy consumption in the UK.* July 2002

DTI. *Energy – its impact on the environment and society.* July 2002

Electricity Association. *Environmental Briefing Number 10: Controlling Atmospheric Emissions from Fossil Fuel Power Stations.* December 2002

Electricity Association. *Environmental Briefing Number 7: Renewable Electricity in the United Kingdom.* August 2000

Electricity Association. *Environmental Briefing Number 13: Transporting Electricity.* February 1999

Electricity Association. *Environmental Briefing Number 18: End-use Energy Efficiency.* June 2000

National Energy Action. *Energy in the Home.* (3rd ed). 1996

Going Green. *Which?*, February 2002, pp 21–3

Solar Heating. *Which?*, March 2002, pp 52–3

Chapter 3 Saving energy

Building Research Establishment. *General Information Leaflet 59: Central Heating System Specifications (CheSS)*

Building Research Establishment. *Good Practice Guide 301 (Domestic heating and hot water: a choice of fuel and system type)*

Department for Environment, Food and Rural Affairs (Defra). *The Government's Standard Assessment Procedure for Energy Rating of Dwellings*. Published on behalf of Defra by BRECSU, BRE. 2001

Department of the Environment, Transport and Regions (DETR). *C: Issuing SAP. Energy and Environmental Best Practice Division*. 2000

Energy Efficiency Partnership for Homes. *If you are replacing domestic heating boilers or hot water vessels you need to know about the new Building Regulations – Part L1*. 2002

Energy Saving Trust. *The DIY Guide to Energy Efficiency*. 2000

Energy Saving Trust. *Is Your Home Behaving Badly?* 2001

Energy Saving Trust. *The Little Blue Book of Boilers* (6th ed). 2002

Energy Saving Trust. *New Building Regulations Will Affect Your Home*. 2002

Harland, E. *Eco-Renovation – The ecological home improvement guide*. Green Books Ltd, 1993

Holloway, D. *The Which? Book of Plumbing & Central Heating*. Which? Books, 2001

National Energy Action. *Energy in the Home*. (3rd ed). 1996

Chapter 4 Household appliances and energy efficiency

Caledonian Magazines. *The Red Book – The Independent Electrical Retailer's Advanced Sales Training Guide*. 2002

Energy Inform. *The Energy Advice Handbook* (3rd ed). 2003

Avoiding a Breakdown. *Which?*, February 1998, pp 8–13

Clean Plates at a Lick. *Which?*, January 1999, pp 38–41

Cookers – choice on the menu. *Which?*, June 1998, pp 28–31

Cool Operators. *Which?*, June 1996, pp 30–34

Fridge-freezers: the chilling facts. *Which?*, October 1997, pp 34–38

Frozen Out. *Which?*, July 1998, pp 38–41

Having a Few Friends Round for Christmas? *Which?*, December 2002, pp 22–25

Hey, Good Looking . . . *Which?*, February 2002, pp 20–23

Inner Spin. *Which?*, November 1997, pp 32–35

Something's Cooking. *Ethical Consumer*. April/May 2002

Time for a Change. *Which?*, June 2002, pp 26–29

Washing Machines. *Which?*, February 1998, pp 40–44

Chapter 5 Water

Borer, P. et al. *The Whole House Book*. Centre for Alternative Technology, 1998

Campbell, S. *The Home Water Supply*. Storey Books, 2000

Harland, E. *Eco-Renovation – The ecological home improvement guide*. Green Books Ltd, 1993

Harper, P. *Water Efficiency in the Home*. CAT (Source: *Clean Slate 28* Spring 1998)

Holloway, D. *The Which? Book of Plumbing and Central Heating*. Which? Books, 2000

Stauffer, J. *The Water Crisis*. Earthscan, 1998

Three Valleys Water. *Where's your water going? A practical guide to tracking down excess water usage*

Go With the Flow. *Which?*, August 1997

Chapter 6 Conservation in the garden

British Permaculture Association. *The Permaculture Plot*

Chase Organics and HDRA. *Organic Gardening Catalogue*

Dobbs, L. *The Gardening Which? Guide to Growing Your Own Vegetables*. Which? Books, 2002

Gardening Which? and the Environment Agency. *Recycled Products for the Garden*. 2002

HDRA. *Composting – A Step-by-Step Organic Gardening Guide*

HDRA. *A Simple Guide to Organic Gardening*. 2000

HDRA. *Step by Step Organic Gardening. Making Worm Compost*. 1992

Waste Watch. *UK Recycled Products Guide*

Whitefield, P. *Permaculture In A Nutshell* (2nd ed). Permaculture Resources, 2000

Conserving Water. *Gardening Which?*, July 1992, pp 218–221

Creating a Wild Corner. *Gardening Which?*, September/October 1988, pp 296–299

Easy Ways to Water. *Gardening Which?*, June 1996, pp 215–217

Making Plants Easy to Water. *Gardening Which?*, July 1997, pp 246–247

Making Waste Work. *Gardening Which?*, August 1999, pp 248–250

Recycled Water. *Gardening Which?*, July 1995, pp 250–252

Recycled Water Features. *Gardening Which?*, July 1997, pp 251–255
Wash . . . and Water! *Gardening Which?*, July 1998, pp 266–267
Waste Free Watering. *Gardening Which?*, July 1997, pp 272–273
Water Saving Ways. *Gardening Which?*, May 1999, pp 175—179
Water-Wise Gardening. *Gardening Which?*, June 2000, pp 249–250
Water When You Want It. *Gardening Which?*, June 1999, pp 246–249
When Organic Is Best. *Gardening Which?*, July 1997, pp 268–270

Chapter 7 Recycling and waste disposal

Friends of the Earth. *Wasted Times* (factsheet)
Women's Environmental Network. *Nappies and the Environment* (factsheet). December 2000
Which? Books. *You and the Environment*. 1990

The Bottom Line: washable nappies. *Which?*, November 2002, pp 30–32
Cold Store. *Which?*, April 2002, pp 42–45
Going Spare. *Which?*, February 2003, pp 27–29
How Green is your Shopping? *Which?*, October 1999, pp 12–15
Nappies – the bottom line. *Ethical Consumer*, February/March 1999, pp 18–19
Recycling: not just a load of rubbish. *Which?*, July 2002, pp 34–36

Chapter 8 Making a difference

Centre for Alternative Technology. *Environmental Building at CAT* (factsheet)
Horne, B. and Geddes, P. *Tapping the Sun: A Guide to Solar Water Heating*. Centre for Alternative Technology, 2000
Trimby, P. *Solar Water Heating: A DIY Guide*. Centre for Alternative Technology, 2000

Solar Heating. *Which?*, March 2002, pp 52–53

Appendix II: Financial help with energy efficiency

Defra. *The Warm Front Team – A Government Funded Initiative*. 2002
Solent Energy Efficiency Advice Centre. *Solent EEAC Grant Finder*. 2002
Solent Energy Efficiency Advice Centre. *Current List of Electricity Tariffs and Offerings Accredited under Future Energy*. 2002

Useful contacts

General

Association for Environment Conscious Building (AECB)
PO Box 32
Llandysul SA44 5ZA
Tel: (01559) 370908
Helpline: (0845) 456 9773 (local rate)
Email: info@aecb.net
Websites: www.aecb.net;
www.newbuilder.co.uk

Association of Plumbing and Heating Contractors (APHC)
14 Ensign House
Ensign Business Centre
Westwood Way
Coventry CV4 8JA
Tel: (0800) 542 6060
Fax: (024) 7647 0942
Email: enquiries@aphc.co.uk
Websites:
www.licensedplumber.co.uk;
www.aphc.co.uk

British Permaculture Association
BCM Permaculture Association
London WC1N 3XX
Tel: (0845) 458 1805;
(0113) 230 7461 (10–2 Tue, Wed, Thur; answerphone at other times)
Email:
office@permaculture.org.uk
Website:
www.permaculture.org.uk

British Wind Energy Association
Renewable Energy House
1 Aztec Row
Berners Road
London N1 0PW
Tel: 020-7689 1960
Fax: 020-7689 1969
Email: info@bwea.com
Websites: www.bwea.com;
www.offshorewindfarms.co.uk

Building Research Establishment (BRE)
Bucknalls Lane
Garston
Watford WD25 9XX
Tel: (01923) 664000
Email: enquiries@bre.co.uk
Website: www.bre.co.uk
Housing Energy Efficiency Best Practice programme:
Tel: (01923) 664258
Email:
enquiries@housingenergy.org.uk
Website:
www.housingenergy.org.uk

Centre for Alternative Technology (CAT)
Machynlleth
Powys SY20 9AZ
Tel: (01654) 705950
Fax: (01654) 702782
Email: info@cat.org.uk
Website: www.cat.org.uk

Centre for Sustainable Energy
The CREATE Centre
Smeaton Road
Bristol BS1 6XN
Tel: 0117-929 9950
Fax: 0117-929 9114
Email: cse@cse.org.uk
Website: www.cse.org.uk

Chase Organics
Riverdene Business Park
Molesey Road
Hersham
Surrey KT12 4RG
Tel: (01932) 253666
Fax: (01932) 252707
Email: richard.rixson@
chaseorganics.co.uk
Website:
www.chaseorganics.co.uk

The Composting Association
Avon House
Tithe Barn Road
Wellingborough
Northamptonshire NN8 1DH
Email: info@compost.org.uk
Website: www.compost.org.uk

Computer Aid
433 Holloway Road
London N7 6LJ
Tel: (0870) 7636 6161 (local rate)
Email: info@computeraid.org
Website: www.computeraid.org

Computers for Charity
PO Box 48
Bude
Cornwall EX23 8BL
Tel: (01288) 361199
Fax: (01288) 361154
Website:
www.computersforcharity.org.uk

Construction Resources
16 Great Guildford Street
London SE1 0HS
Tel: 020-7450 2211
Fax: 020-7450 2212
Email: sales@ecoconstruct.com
Website:
www.constructionresources.com

**Department for Environment,
Food and Rural Affairs (Defra)**
Ergon House
17 Smith Square
London SW1P 3JR
Tel: (0845) 933 5577
Minicom/textphone:
(0845) 300 1998
Fax: 020-7238 3329
Email: helpline@defra.gsi.gov.uk
Websites: www.defra.gov.uk;
www.doingyourbit.org.uk

**Department of Trade and
Industry (DTI)**
Enquiry Unit
1 Victoria Street
London SW1H 0ET
Tel: 020-7215 5000
Minicom: 020-7215 6740
Website: www.dti.gov.uk

Drinking Water Inspectorate
Floor 2/A1
Ashdown House
123 Victoria Street
London SW1E 6DE
Tel: 020-7944 5956
Fax: 020-7944 5969
Email:
dwi.enquiries@defra.gsi.gov.uk
Website: www.dwi.gov.uk

**Electrical Contractors' Association
(ECA)**
ESCA House
34 Palace Court
London W2 4HY
Tel: 020-7313 4800
Website: www.eca.co.uk

Elemental Solutions
Herefordshire office:
Withy Cottage
Little Hill
Orcop
Hereford HR2 8SE
Tel: (01981) 540728
Fax: (01981) 541044
Email: nick.es@aecb.net
Website:
www.elementalsolutions.co.uk

Gloucestershire office:
Oaklands Park
Newnham
Gloucestershire GL14 1EF
Tel: (01594) 516063
Fax: (01594) 516821
Email: mark.es@aecb.net
Website: as above

Energy Saving Trust (EST)
21 Dartmouth Street
London SW1H 9BP
Tel: 020-7222 0101
Helpline: (0845) 727 7200
Fax: 020-7654 2444
Email: info@est.co.uk
Websites: www.est.org.uk
(corporate information);
www.saveenergy.co.uk
(consumer information)
See later in this section for a list of Energy Efficiency Advice Centres (EEACs). Call your local EEAC to access the Energy Efficiency Installer Network

Energywatch
4th Floor
Artillery House
Artillery Row
London SW1P 1RT
Tel: (0845) 906 0708
Fax: 020-7799 8341
Email:
enquiries@energywatch.org.uk
Website:
www.energywatch.org.uk

Environment Agency
General enquiry line: (0845) 933
3111 (to be put you through to
your local office)
Emergency hotline: (0800)
807060 (for emergencies, such as
reporting a pollution incident)
Floodline: (0845) 988 1188 (for
information on flooding)
Email: enquiries@environment-
agency.gov.uk
Website: www.environment-
agency.gov.uk
To order a copy of Recycled
Products for the Garden *(listed as*
Recycling in the Garden*) call the
general enquiry line*

Ethical Consumer *magazine*
Unit 21
41 Old Birley Street
Manchester M15 5RF
Tel: 0161-226 2929
Fax: 0161-226 6277
Email:
mail@ethicalconsumer.org
Website:
www.ethicalconsumer.org

Forest Stewardships Council (FSC)
Unit D
Station Buildings
Llanidloes
Powys SY18 6EB
Tel: (01686) 413916
Fax: (01686) 412176
Email: info@fsc-uk.org
Website: www.fsc-uk.info

Friends of the Earth (FoE)
26–28 Underwood Street
London N1 7JQ
Tel: 020-7490 1555
Fax: 020-7490 0881
Email: info@foe.co.uk
Website: www.foe.co.uk

Furniture Recycling Network
Wakefield CFS
The Old Drill Hall
17a Vicarage Street North
Wakefield
West Yorkshire WF1 4JS
Tel: (01924) 375252
Fax: (01924) 375252
Email: furniture.rn@virgin.net
Website:
www.reuze.co.uk/furniture.shtml

Gaia Energy Centre
Delabole
North Cornwall PL33 9DA
Tel: (01840) 213321
Fax: (01840) 213428
Email: info@gaiaenergy.co.uk
Website: www.gaiaenergy.co.uk

Gardening Which?
PO Box 44
Hertford SG14 1SH
Tel: (0800) 252100
Email: gardening@which.net
Website:
www.which.net/gardeningwhich
For a copy of Recycled Products
for the Garden *call (0845) 903
7000 quoting RECPRO*

Global Action Plan (GAP)
8 Fulwood Place
London WC1V 6HG
Tel: 020-7405 5633
Fax: 020-7831 6244
Email: all@gapuk.demon.co.uk
Website:
www.globalactionplan.org.uk

Green Choices
PO Box 31617
London SW2 4FF
Email: info@greenchoices.org
Website: www.greenchoices.org

The Green Directory
58 Kingley Close
Wickford
Essex SS12 0EN
Tel: (01268) 468000
Fax: (01268) 451111
Email: info@greendirectory.net
Website: www.greendirectory.net

Green Guide Publishing Ltd
PO Box 17568
London N1 2WQ
Tel/Fax: 020-8815 4730
Email: sales@greenguide.co.uk.
Website:
www.greenguideonline.com

Greenpeace
Canonbury Villas
London N1 2PN
Tel: 020-7865 8100
Fax: 020-7865 8200
Email: info@uk.greenpeace.org
Website: www.greenpeace.org.uk

Heating and Ventilating Contractors' Association (HVCA)
ESCA House
34 Palace Court
London W2 4JG
Tel: 020-7313 4900
Fax: 020-7727 9268
Email: contact@hvca.org.uk
Website: www.hvca.org.uk

Hedgehog Self-Build Co-op
Hogs Edge, Brighton
Website:
www.sustainablehomes.co.uk/
case_studies/hedgehog.htm
Contact:
Robin Hillier
Walter Segal Self-Build Trust
15 High Street
Belford
Northumberland NE70 7NG
Tel: (01668) 213544
Fax: (01668) 219247
Email: info@segalselfbuild.co.uk
Website:
www.segalselfbuild.co.uk
See also Sustainable Homes

HDRA, The Organic Organisation
HDRA National Centre for
Organic Gardening
Ryton Organic Gardens
Coventry
Warwickshire CV8 3LG
Tel: (02476) 303517
Fax: (02476) 639228
Email: enquiry@dhra.org.uk
Website: www.hdra.org.uk

Institute of Plumbing (IoP)
64 Station Lane
Hornchurch
Essex RM12 6NB
Tel: (01708) 472791
Fax: (01708) 448987
Email: info@plumbers.org.uk
Website: www.plumbers.org.uk

INTEGER (Intelligent and Green) Ltd
Building 9
Bucknalls Lane
Garston
Watford WD25 9XX
Tel: (01923) 665955
Fax: (01923) 665956
Email:
integer@integerproject.co.uk
Website:
www.integerproject.co.uk

Intergovernmental Panel on Climate Change (IPCC)
IPCC Secretariat
c/o World Meteorological
Organization
7bis Avenue de la Paix
C.P. 2300, CH-1211
Geneva 2
Switzerland
Tel: (+41) 22-730-8208
Fax: (+41) 22-730-8025
Email:
ipcc_sec@gateway.wmo.ch
Website: www.ipcc.ch

Kings Hill Development
Kings Hill Park
Discovery Drive
Kings Hill
West Malling
Kent
Tel: (01732) 871872
Email:
ctaylor@kingshillpark.co.uk
Website:
www.kingshillpark.co.uk

Living Water
5 Holyrood Road
Edinburgh EH8 8AE
Tel: 0131-558 3313
Fax: 0131-558 1550
Email: hello@livingwater.org.uk
Website: www.livingwater.org.uk

Mailing Preference Service (MPS)
DMA House
70 Margaret Street
London W1W 8SS
Tel: 020-7291 3320
Fax: 020-7323 4226
Email: mps@dma.org.uk
Website:
www.mps-online.org.uk
(to register free of charge)

National Association of Nappy Services (NANS)
Tel: 0121-693 4949
Email:
info@changeanappy.co.uk
Website:
www.changeanappy.co.uk
Call NANS to find out the location of your nearest nappy laundry service. They supply everything you need, and sterilise nappies to NHS hygiene standards

National Energy Action (NEA)
National Office
St Andrew's House
90–92 Pilgrim Street
Newcastle upon Tyne NE1 6SG
Tel: 0191-261 5677
Fax: 0191-261 6496
Email: info@nea.org.uk
Website: www.nea.org.uk

The National Energy Foundation
See The National Energy Centre

The National Energy Centre
Davy Avenue
Knowlhill
Milton Keynes MK5 8NG
Tel: (01908) 665555
Fax: (01908) 665577
Email: nef@natenergy.org.uk
Website: www.natenergy.org.uk

NEF Renewables
The National Energy Centre
Address as previous page
Tel: (01908) 665555; (0800) 138
0889
Fax: (01908) 665577
Email:
renewables@greenenergy.org.uk
Website:
www.greenenergy.org.uk

National Grid Transco
31 Homer Road
Solihull
West Midlands B91 3LT
Tel: 0121-626 4431
Website: www.transco.uk.com

National Home Energy Rating (NHER)
The National Energy Centre
Address as previous page
Tel: (01908) 672787
Fax: (01908) 662296
Email: enquiry@nesltd.co.uk
Website: www.nher.co.uk

National Inspection Council for Electrical Installation Contractors (NICEIC)
Vintage House
37 Albert Embankment
London SE1 7UJ
Tel: 020-7564 2323
Fax: 020-7564 2370
Technical helpline: 020-7564 2320
Website: www.niceic.org.uk

National Insulation Association (NIA)
PO Box 12
Haslemere
Surrey GU27 3AH
Tel: (01428) 654011
Fax: (01428) 651401
Email: insulationassoc@aol.com
Website:
www.insulationassociation.org.uk

National Trust
Membership Department
PO Box 39
Bromley
Kent BR1 3XL
Tel: (0870) 458 4000
Minicom: (0870) 240 3207
Fax: 020-8466 6824
Email:
enquiries@thenationaltrust.org.uk
Website:
www.nationaltrust.org.uk

The Nottingham Ecohome
Penney Poyzer & Gil Schalom
9 Patrick Road
West Bridgford
Nottingham
Email gil@msarch.co.uk
Website:
www.msarch.co.uk/ecohome

Office of Gas and Electricity
Markets (OFGEM)
9 Millbank
London SW1P 3GE
Tel: 020-7901 7000
Fax: 020-7901 7066
Website: www.ofgem.gov.uk
or:
Regents Court
70 West Regent Street
Glasgow G2 2QZ
Tel: 0141-331 2678
Fax: 0141-331 2777
Website: as above

Office of Water Services
(OFWAT)
Centre City Tower
7 Hill Street
Birmingham B5 4UA
Tel: 0121-625 1300
Fax: 0121-625 1400
Email:
enquiries@ofwat.gsi.gov.uk
Website: www.ofwat.gov.uk

Peabody Trust Housing
Association
45 Westminster Bridge Road
London SE1 7JB
Tel: 020-7928 7811
Fax: 020-7261 9187
Email: pr@peabody.org.uk
Website: www.peabody.org.uk

Real Nappy Association (RNA)
PO Box 3704
London SE26 4RX
Tel: 020-8299 4519
Email: contact@realnappy.com
Website: www.realnappy.com
The Real Nappy Project *is a joint*
Women's Environmental
Network/Real Nappy Association
campaign, and a central source of
information and advice on all nappy-
related issues. For a free parents'
information pack (including a list of
suppliers) send a large SAE with two
stamps attached. Alternatively, visit
www.wen.org.uk

Royal Horticultural Society
Administrative Offices, Lindley
Library and Exhibition Halls
80 Vincent Square
London SW1P 2PE
Tel: 020-7834 4333
Fax: 020-7821 3020
Email: info@rhs.org.uk
Website: www.rhs.org.uk

Scottish Water
55 Buckstone Terrace
Edinburgh EH10 6XH
Tel: (0845) 601 8855
Email: customerservice@
scottishwater.co.uk
Website:
www.scottishwater.co.uk

Solid Fuel Association
7 Swanwick Court
Alfreton
Derbyshire DE55 7AS
Helpline: (0845) 601 4406
Fax: (01773) 834351
Email: sfa@solidfuel.co.uk
Website: www.solidfuel.co.uk

Sustainable Homes
7 High Street
Harlequin House
Teddington
Middlesex GW11 8EE
Tel: 020-8943 4433
Website:
www.sustainablehomes.co.uk

The Tank Exchange
Lewden House
Barnsley Road
Dodworth
Barnsley
South Yorkshire S75 3JU
Tel: (08704) 670706
Fax: (08704) 671685
Email: raintanks@aol.co.uk
Website:
www.thetankexchange.com

UK Climate Impacts Programme
Union House
12–16 St Michael's Street
Oxford OX1 2DU
Tel: (01865) 432076
Fax: (01865) 432077
Email: enquiries@ukcip.org.uk
Website: ukcip.org.uk

Waste Watch
96 Tooley Street
London SE1 2TH
Tel: 020-7089 2100
Wasteline: (0870) 243 0136
Fax: 020-7403 4802
Email: info@wastewatch.org.uk
Website:
www.wastewatch.org.uk

WaterVoice
Centre City Tower
7 Hill Street
Birmingham B5 4UA
Email:
enquiries@watervoice.org.uk
Website: www.watervoice.org.uk

Water UK
1 Queen Anne's Gate
London SW1H 9BT
Tel: 020-7344 1844
Fax: 020-7344 1866
Website: www.water.org.uk

The Water Service
Tel: (0845) 744 0088
Email:
waterline@waterni.gov.uk
Website: www.waterni.gov.uk

Which? Books
PO Box 44
Hertford SG14 1SH
Tel: (0800) 252100
Email: books@which.net
Website: www.which.net

Women's Environmental Network (WEN)
PO Box 30626
London E1 1TZ
Tel: 020-7481 9004
Fax: 020-7481 9144
Email: info@wen.org.uk
Website: www.wen.org.uk

Energy Efficiency Advice Centres (EEACs)

General helpline: (0800) 512012

Aberdeen & North East
1 Cotton Street
Aberdeen AB11 5EE
Tel: (01224) 253919
Email: info@scarf.org.uk

Anglia East
c/o Broadland District Council
1 Yarmouth Road
Norwich NR7 0DU
Tel: (01603) 703975
Email: ange@eeac.net

Anglia West
33A Westgate
Peterborough PE1 1PZ
Tel: (01733) 566553
Email: angw@eeac.net

Bedfordshire & Hertfordshire
Room 236
South Bedfordshire District Council
The District Offices
High Street North
Dunstable LU6 1LF
Tel: (01582) 474191
Email: beds@eeac.net

Belfast
1–11 May Street
Belfast
Northern Ireland BT1 4NA
Tel: (028) 9024 0664
Email: belf@eeac.net

Black Country
Sandwell New Horizons Building
Kelvin Way
West Bromwich
West Midlands B70 7JW
Tel: 0121-553 7600
Email: bceeac@savenergy.org

Bristol & Somerset
The Centre for Sustainable Energy
Create Centre
Smeaton Road
Bristol BS1 6XN
Tel: (0117) 929 9404
Email: advice@cse.org.uk

Carlisle & County
Carlisle City Council
Civic Centre
Carlisle CA3 8QG
Tel: (01228) 817497
Email: carl@eeac.net

Central Midlands
Room 120/122
Gazette Building
168 Corporation Street
Birmingham B4 6TF
Tel: 0121-200 1339
Email: cmeeac@savenergy.org

Cheshire
Rooms 2–4
Brunner Guildhall
High Street
Winsford
Cheshire CW7 2AU
Tel: (01606) 594132
Email: ches@eeac.net

Cornwall
2 The Setons
Tolvaddon Energy Park
Camborne
Cornwall TR14 0HX
Tel: (01209) 614975
Email: advice@cap.org.uk

Devon
4th floor
Royal Building
11 St Andrews Cross
Plymouth PL1 1DN
Tel: (01752) 235187
Email:
info@devon-energy-advice.org

Dorset & Wiltshire
CSE
PO Box 5138
Bournemouth BH11 8XZ
Tel: (0117) 929 9404
Email: dors@eeac.net

Essex
16 Bentalls Shopping Centre
Colchester Road
Heybridge
Essex CM9 4GD
Tel: (01621) 853862
Email: info@essexeeac.com

Gloucestershire
Unit 6/15
The MEWs
Brook Street
Mitcheldean
Gloucestershire GL17 0SL
Tel: (01594) 544124
Email: glou@eeac.net

Greater Manchester North
18 Union Street
Oldham OL1 1BD
Tel: 0161-626 9347
Email: gman@eeac.net

Greater Manchester South
4th floor
Basil House
105–107 Portland Street
Manchester M1 6DF
Tel: 0161-242 5819
Email:
eeac@manchester.city.council

Highland
Energy and Engineering Section
The Highland Council
Kinmylies Building
Leachkin Road
Inverness IV3 8NN
Tel: (01463) 703500
Email: high@eeac.net

Kent
3rd floor
International House
Dover Place
Ashford
Kent TN23 1UH
Tel: 020-8683 6644
Email: kent@eeac.net

Kirklees, Calderdale & Wakefield
Kirklees Energy Services
12 Byram Buildings
Station Street
Huddersfield
West Yorkshire HD1 1LS
Tel: (01484) 351550
Email: info@energy-help.org.uk

Lancashire
The Hothouse
32 Addison Close
Blackburn
Lancashire BB2 1QU
Tel: (01254) 698167
Email: lanc@eeac.net

Leeds Bradford Hull
Leeds City Council
Neighbourhoods and Housing
Department
Selectapost 12
Thoresby House
2A Great George Street
Leeds LS2 8BB
Tel: (0113) 214 5154
Email: leed@eeac.net

**Leicestershire &
Northamptonshire**
2–4 Market Place South
Leicester LE1 5HB
Tel: (0115) 918 2901
Email:
leicleac@leicleac.demon.co.uk

Lincolnshire
East Lindsey District Council
Offices
Tedder Hall
Manby Park
Louth
Lincolnshire LN11 8UP
Tel: (01507) 329488
Email: linc@eeac.net

Lothian & Edinburgh
36 Newhaven Road
Edinburgh EH6 5PY
Tel: 0131-555 4008
Email:
advice@edinleac.demon.co.uk

Merseyside
Manor Trust Building
79 Gorsey Lane
Wallasey
Wirral CH44 4HF
Tel: 0151-639 9499
Email: mers@eeac.net

Mid- and South-west Wales
West Wales Eco Centre
Lower St Mary Street
Newport
Pembrokeshire SA42 0TS
Tel: (01239) 820156
Email:
advice@leacwest.demon.co.uk

MK, Bucks & East Berks
The National Energy Centre
Davy Avenue
Knowlhill
Milton Keynes MK5 8NG
Tel: (01908) 665566
Email: milt@eeac.net

North-east London
31 Church Hill
Walthamstow
London E17 3RU
Tel: 020-8521 3156
Email: nelo@eeac.net

North Wales
The Town Hall
Earl Road
Mold
Flintshire CH7 1AB
Tel: (01352) 755981
Email: advice@nweeac.fsnet.co.uk

North-west London
Islington Energy Centre
159 Upper Street
London N1 1RE
Tel: 020-7527 2121
Email:
energy.advice@islington.gov.uk

Northern & Western Isles
26 Bridge Street
Kirkwall
Orkney KW15 1HR
Tel: (01856) 870534
Email: ken@orkleac.demon.co.uk

Northumbria
9–10 Charlotte Square
Newcastle upon Tyne NE1 4XF
Tel: (0191) 233 2566
Email:
northeeac@btconnect.com

Nottinghamshire & Derbyshire
30 Market Street
Buxton
Derbyshire SK17 6LD
Tel: (01298) 71342
Email:
energyadvice@highpeak.gov.uk

Shropshire, Hereford & Stoke
Jubilee House
74 High Street
Madeley
Telford
Shropshire TF7 5AH
Tel: (01952) 272042
Email: toni@telfleac.demon.co.uk

Solent
The Environment Centre
14–15 Brunswick Place
Southampton SO15 2AQ
Tel: (02380) 234288

South-east London
Room 400
Town Hall
Catford Road
London SE6 4RU
Tel: 020-8314 6339
Email: selo@eeac.net

South-east Wales
Terminus Building
Wood Street
Cardiff CF10 1EQ
Tel: (02920) 231245
Email: sewa@eeac.net

South Yorkshire
PO Box 257
Floor 3
The Council House
College Road
Doncaster DN1 1RN
Tel: (01302) 737036
Email: syor@eeac.net

South-west London
CEN
Ambassador House
Brigstock Road
Thornton Heath
Surrey CR7 7JG
Tel: 020-8683 6634
Email: swlo@eeac.net

South-west Scotland
9 High Street
Ayr KA7 1LU
Tel: (01292) 280109
Email: energy.agency@
southayrshire.gov.uk

Strathclyde & Central
72 Charlotte Street
Glasgow G1 5DW
Tel: 0141-552 0799
Email:
advice@glasleac.demon.co.uk

Surrey & East Sussex
Unit 327
30 Great Guildford Street
London SE1 0HS
Tel: 020-7922 1668
Email: advice@ecsc.org.uk

Tayside
SCARF
Ridgeway House
Balgray Place
Dundee DD3 8SH
Tel: (01382) 889673
Email: tays@eeac.net

Tees & Durham
Tees & Durham Energy
Efficiency Advice (TADEA)
6 Belasis Court
Belasis Hall
Technology Park
Bellingham
TS23 4AZ
Tel: (01642) 373020
Email: advice@tadea.com

Thames & Central London
1 Old Town Hall
Polytechnic Street
Woolwich
London SE18 6PN
Tel: 020-8855 5533
Email: thcl@eeac.net

Thames Valley
WODC Building
Avenue 4
Station Lane
Witney
Oxfordshire OX28 4BN
Tel: (01993) 709688
Email: energy.advice@tvec.org.uk

Warwickshire, Worcestershire
& Coventry
Wellesbourne House
Walton Road
Wellesbourne
Warwickshire CV35 9JB
Tel: (01789) 842898
Email: warw@eeac.net

West Sussex
PO Box 558
Crawley RH10 1WY
Tel: (01293) 438950
Email: wsus@eeac.net

Western Regional
1 Nugents Entry
Off Town Hall Street
Enniskillen
County Fermanagh BT74 7DF
Tel: (02866) 328269
Email: all@wrean.co.uk

York, North Yorkshire &
East Riding
20 George Hudson Street
York YO1 6WR
Tel: (01904) 554406
Email: york@eeac.net

Useful websites

www.bedzed.org.uk
Beddington Zero Energy
Development

www.boilers.org.uk Boiler
efficiency technical database

www.buy.co.uk To compare
utility suppliers and costs,
including the cost of metered
water

www.centralheating.co.uk
The Central Heating Information
Council

www.commonground.org.uk
Campaigning group for local
environment and community

www.cse.org.uk Centre for
Sustainable Energy – working
with local government to
promote energy efficiency

www.defra.gov.uk/
environment/consumerprod/
gcc The government's 'Green
Claims Code'

www.doingyourbit.org.uk
Government tips for recycling
and improving the environment

www.dti.gov.uk/energy The
Department of Trade and
Industry's Energy Group product
information and guidance

www.earthwatch.org Conservation through research and education

www.energy-plus.org Europe-wide resource on energy-efficient cold appliances

www.energy.org.uk Understanding Energy – the educational service of the major UK energy companies

www.energywatch.org.uk The independent gas and electricity consumer watchdog (includes details of price-comparison websites)

www.ethical-junction.org Ethical services, suppliers and virtual 'shopping village'

www.foe.co.uk Friends of the Earth

www.futureforests.com Tree planting scheme to offset carbon dioxide emissons

www.globalactionplan.org.uk Practical solutions to environmental and social problems

www.greenbuildingstore.co.uk Sustainable building products (supplier)

www.greenconstruction.co.uk 'Green' building information resource

www.greendirectory.net Listings of 'green' shops, companies and suppliers

www.greenpeace.org.uk Greenpeace

www.greenprices.co.uk Price calculator and information on 'green' energy suppliers

www.groundwork.org.uk Local environmental regeneration through partnerships

www.icer.org.uk Industry information on recycling electrical and electronic equipment

www.livingearth.org.uk Environmental education and community development programmes

www.livingwater.org.uk Ecological principles applied to a range of water and waste problems for households, agriculture and industry

www.mtprog.com Market Transformation Programme (MTP) – a strategic policy unit run by Defra to promote greener products, systems and services

www.recycledproducts.org.uk Information on where to buy recycled products, maintained by Waste Watch

www.retra.co.uk Electrical and electronic retailers' trade association, offering information and advice on products

www.saveenergy.co.uk The Energy Saving Trust's consumer information website

www.switchwithwhich.co.uk For advice on changing your energy supplier

www.3valleys.co.uk Three Valleys Water (supplier)

www.ukace.org Association for the Conservation of Energy – campaigning organisation

www.ukepic.co.uk The UK Environmental Product Information Consortium

www.wastepoint.co.uk A database of every recycling point in the UK

www.wastewatch.org.uk Promotes action on waste reduction, reuse and recycling; includes a National Recycling Directory

www.watervoice.org.uk Answers to common questions and consumer advice about your water supply

Index

WHICH? BOOKS

The following titles were available as this book went to press.

General reference (legal, financial, practical, etc.)

	pages	price
Be Your Own Financial Adviser	448pp	£10.99
420 Legal Problems Solved	352pp	£9.99
160 Letters that Get Results	352pp	£10.99
Rip-off Britain – and how to beat it	256pp	£5.99
What to Do When Someone Dies	192pp	£9.99
The Which? Computer Troubleshooter	192pp	£12.99
The Which? Guide to Baby Products	240pp	£9.99
The Which? Guide to Changing Careers	352pp	£10.99
The Which? Guide to Choosing a Career	336pp	£9.99
The Which? Guide to Choosing a School	336pp	£10.99
The Which? Guide to Computers	352pp	£10.99
The Which? Guide to Computers for Small Businesses	352pp	£10.99
The Which? Guide to Divorce	368pp	£10.99
The Which? Guide to Doing Your Own Conveyancing	208pp	£9.99
The Which? Guide to Employment	352pp	£11.99
The Which? Guide to the Energy Saving Home	224pp	£10.99
The Which? Guide to Help in the Home	208pp	£9.99
The Which? Guide to Gambling	288pp	£9.99
The Which? Guide to Getting Married	256pp	£10.99
The Which? Guide to Giving and Inheriting	256pp	£9.99
The Which? Guide to Going Digital	272pp	£10.99
The Which? Guide to Insurance	320pp	£10.99
The Which? Guide to the Internet	320pp	£10.99
The Which? Guide to Living Together	192pp	£9.99
The Which? Guide to Money	448pp	£9.99
The Which? Guide to Money in Retirement	288pp	£10.99
The Which? Guide to Money on the Internet	256pp	£9.99

The Which? Guide to Planning Your Pension	368pp	£10.99
The Which? Guide to Renting and Letting	352pp	£11.99
The Which? Guide to Shares	288pp	£9.99
The Which? Guide to Starting Your Own Business	224pp	£10.99
The Which? Guide to Working from Home	304pp	£10.99
Which? Way to Buy, Own and Sell a Flat	352pp	£10.99
Which? Way to Buy, Sell and Move House	320pp	£10.99
Which? Way to Clean It	256pp	£10.99
Which? Way to Drive Your Small Business	240pp	£10.99
Which? Way to Manage Your Time – and Your Life	208pp	£9.99
Which? Way to Save and Invest	336pp	£14.99
Which? Way to Save Tax	242pp	£14.99
Wills and Probate	192pp	£10.99

Make Your Own Will	28pp	£10.99

Action Pack (A5 wallet with forms and 28-page booklet)

Take Control of Your Pension	48pp	£10.99

Action Pack (A5 wallet with calculation sheets and 48-page booklet)

Health

The Which? Guide to Children's Health	288pp	£9.99
The Which? Guide to Complementary Therapies	256pp	£10.99
The Which? Guide to Counselling and Therapy	288pp	£10.99
The Which? Guide to Managing Asthma	256pp	£9.99
The Which? Guide to Managing Back Trouble	160pp	£9.99
The Which? Guide to Managing Stress	304pp	£10.99
The Which? Guide to Men's Health	336pp	£9.99
The Which? Guide to Personal Health	320pp	£10.99
The Which? Guide to Women's Health	448pp	£9.99

Gardening

The Gardening Which? Guide to Growing		
Your Own Vegetables (hardback)	224pp	£18.99
(paperback)	224pp	£12.99
The Gardening Which? Guide to		
Patio and Container Plants	224pp	£17.99
The Gardening Which? Guide to		
Small Gardens	224pp	£12.99
The Gardening Which? Guide to		
Successful Perennials	224pp	£12.99
The Gardening Which? Guide to		
Successful Propagation	160pp	£12.99
The Gardening Which? Guide to		
Successful Pruning	240pp	£12.99
The Gardening Which? Guide to		
Successful Shrubs	224pp	£12.99

Do-it-yourself

The Which? Book of		
Plumbing and Central Heating	160pp	£13.99
The Which? Book of Wiring and Lighting	160pp	£16.99
Which? Way to Fix It	208pp	£12.99

Travel/leisure

The Good Bed and Breakfast Guide 2003	624pp	£14.99
The Good Food Guide	768pp	£15.99
The Good		
Skiing and Snowboarding Guide	384pp	£15.99
The Which? Guide to Country Pubs	576pp	£14.99
The Which? Guide to Pub Walks	256pp	£9.99
The Which? Guide to Scotland	528pp	£12.99
The Which? Guide to Tourist Attractions	544pp	£12.99
The Which? Guide to		
Weekend Breaks in Britain	528pp	£13.99
The Which? Hotel Guide	704pp	£15.99
The Which? Wine Guide	544pp	£14.99
Which? Holiday Destination	624pp	£12.99

Available from bookshops, and by post from:
Which?, Dept BKLIST, Castlemead,
Gascoyne Way, Hertford X, SG14 1LH
or phone FREE on (0800) 252100
quoting Dept BKLIST and your credit card details